Andrew D. Mayes is Adviser for Spirituality and a parish priest in the Diocese of Chichester. He has lived in Jerusalem for some years, latterly as Course Director of St George's College. He is the author of *Spirituality in Ministerial Formation* (University of Wales Press), as well as *Holy Land?*, *Spirituality of Struggle* and *Celebrating the Christian Centuries* (all SPCK).

BEYOND THE EDGE

*Spiritual transitions for
adventurous souls*

Andrew D. Mayes

First published in Great Britain in 2013

Society for Promoting Christian Knowledge
36 Causton Street
London SW1P 4ST
www.spckpublishing.co.uk

British Library Cataloguing-in-Publication Data
A catalogue record for this book is available from the British Library

ISBN 978–0–281–07114–2
eBook ISBN 978–0–281–07115–9

eBook by Graphicraft Limited, Hong Kong

Typeset by Graphicraft Limited, Hong Kong
First printed in Great Britain by Ashford Colour Press
Subsequently digitally printed in Great Britain

Produced on paper from sustainable forests

Contents

—•◆•—

Introduction   vii

1 Wading across the river   1

2 Advancing through desert margins   13

3 Venturing to the coastlands   24

4 Traversing the risky lake   40

5 Penetrating Samaria's border   56

6 Climbing the mountain of encounter   68

7 Discovering the forgotten threshold   80

8 Ascending towards the holy city   91

9 Passing over   100

10 Reaching beyond limits   111

Appendix: Models of spiritual direction and accompaniment   120

Notes   135

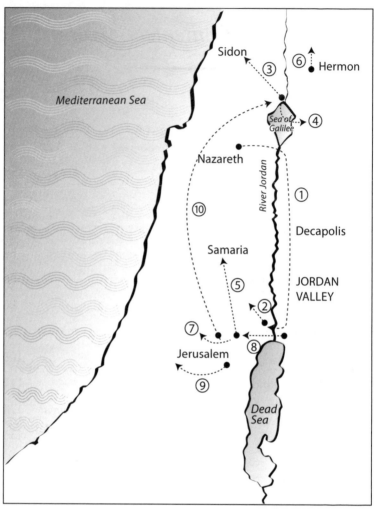

●·········▶ = Journey of Jesus

① From Galilee to the Jordan Valley   ⑥ Up Mt Hermon

② Into the desert   ⑦ Across Siloam to Jerusalem

③ From Galilee to Sidon   ⑧ From the desert to the Mt of Olives

④ Across the Sea of Galilee   ⑨ From Gethsemane to Calvary

⑤ From Jerusalem to Samaria   ⑩ From Jerusalem to Galilee

Introduction

From across the centuries the summons reverberates in our souls today: 'Follow Me!' And where does Jesus go, that we might follow? He leads his disciples, then and now, into dangerous, demanding and life-transforming spaces. This book aims to bring together in a dynamic interplay three key ideas: the journeys of Jesus in the Gospels, where he is leading his disciples into risky locations; the concept of liminality or crossing a threshold to a new place of discovery; and the movements and transitions that might happen to us as we pray and advance in our adventure of discipleship. It is written for those unafraid to explore risky places in their odyssey of prayer: for seekers, for spiritual directors or those who walk with others in their prayer journey. It is for those who would call themselves pilgrims and wayfarers on a spiritual quest. Its aim is to stimulate and resource the journey. Let's look at the three big concepts in turn.

Jesus in motion

Soon after the resurrection, according to the Acts of the Apostles, Peter describes and sums up in a vivid, startling phrase his experience with Jesus. He refers to 'the time that the Lord Jesus went in and out among us' (Acts 1.21). This phrase captures the dynamic of Jesus' journeys. He was always crossing boundaries, in and out of one place or another.

One of the things that struck me when I was working in the Holy Land as Course Director of St George's College, Jerusalem was this: how often in the Gospels Jesus is in movement, in motion. Jesus in the Gospels is radically itinerant: he doesn't settle down in his three year ministry but is always on the move. Indeed, 'The Son of Man has nowhere to lay his head' (Luke

9.58). Jesus is a pilgrim and wayfarer. According to Matthew's Gospel, Jesus became a traveller and an exile at just a few days old, a refugee, crossing the border into Egypt. Mark's Gospel emphasizes his travels: seven times he uses the phrase 'on the way' – a symbol of the journey of discipleship.[1] In his ministry he is peripatetic, always roving. He says: 'today, tomorrow, and the next day I must be on my way' (Luke 13.33). And he is ever leading his disciples into liminal space: he leads them across borders, through boundaries, into a risky place, where they will be radically changed. This resonates with the figure of Christ the trailblazer, the *archegos* in the Letter to the Hebrews (12.2): Jesus is the pioneer, the forerunner, going on before in order to lead God's people into dangerous but transformative spaces. Now working as Spirituality Adviser to a large diocese, I am noticing afresh how relevant this is to the adventure of our spiritual lives.

In the Gospels we see that Jesus accompanies the disciples across the mountains of the north, to Tyre and Sidon, to the Mediterranean Sea, exposing them not only to the sea breezes but to new horizons in every sense. We see Jesus entering with the disciples the 'no-go' area, the place of heretics called Samaria. Jesus guides the disciples up Mount Hermon to get a glimpse of heaven itself and a sighting of the passion. On his final journey Jesus leads the disciples across the desert of testing – there is no other way from Jericho to Jerusalem except through the desert of the Judean wilderness, the primordial liminal space. Jesus takes his disciples across the numinous threshold of the Mount of Olives, the brink of Jerusalem.

In the Gospels Jesus is ever going places and seeking to take his disciples with him: 'where I am, you shall be also' (John 14.3). When we look at the Gospels, and appreciate the geography of the Holy Land, we see Jesus entering the liminal zone time and again. Sometimes he has to walk alone into this space, but significantly, at other times he takes his disciples with him and hopes the experience will change them radically. This gives fresh meaning to our understanding of the disciple as one who 'follows Jesus'.

Across thresholds, beyond borders

The concept of liminality is inspiring, unsettling and energizing. In entering liminal space you leave behind your former ideals and conventions, the status quo, the ordinary routines, inherited mindsets. You also leave behind your safety zone; you quit your place of security. You step out into a space where you will see things differently, where your world view might be shattered, where your existing priorities might be turned upside down. You cross a border and go beyond your usual limits. What had been a barrier now becomes a threshold, a stepping stone into a larger spiritual adventure. The liminal spaces into which Jesus leads us are places of radical unmaking and unlearning – uncomfortable spaces where we're called to be utterly vulnerable to God, and from which we will re-enter the world quite changed, even converted! The *limen* is the threshold, the place of departure, a springboard into a fresh way of doing things.

The concept of liminality derives from Arnold van Gennep's 1909 study, *Rites de Passage*, an anthropological study of ritual in communities.[2] He identified three stages in a process of transition: **separation**, involving a metaphorical death or breaking with past practices and expectations; **liminal state**, where those to be initiated – for example, young people into adulthood – must face challenges to their sense of identity and a process of re-formation; and **aggregation** or reintegration into the community as a changed person with a sharpened sense of values.

Victor Turner took this further in his studies among tribes in Zambia.[3] He noticed that the transitional phase was a testing process of undoing and remaking. The place of liminality thus becomes a place of ambiguity and confusion as one world is left behind – one thought-world – and things are shaken up before one can re-enter society with a different perspective, indeed a different social status. This is the place of 'anti-structure' – the opposite of the world of normality and of usual structures and roles, the place of status quo, 'business as usual'. But while it is a place of uncertainty, it is precisely here that the person clarifies his or her sense of identity and purpose – things are discovered in the liminal zone that can't be found in the routines of normal life.

Our journey of faith

All this resonates strongly, I think, with our current experience. We find ourselves in a liminal space, right now. We live in an in-between time, betwixt and between. Old paradigms are breaking up, political regimes are in revolution, banking and economic systems are breaking down. In the Church, patterns of ministry are in flux. The parish system is crumbling. Worship and liturgy are being rewritten almost daily.

In postmodern society everything is questioned, no objective truths are to be entertained. We find ourselves in a space where we may long with nostalgia for old, familiar certainties and securities, for the traditional and safe. But we find, instead, that it is *precisely* here, in the risky and dangerous place, that Christ waits to meet us, to reveal himself to us.

As Hauerwas and Willimon have reminded us, we are called to live as aliens, exiles and pilgrims – that is to say, as liminal people – in this present world.[4] With the collapse of Christendom and a Constantinian model of Church and State, we find ourselves in a liminal zone that is bewildering and disorientating. Old familiar landmarks are passing and we are out of our comfort zone. But the liminal place is also the place of discovery, creativity, potentiality. The place of risk is a place of paradox: it is discomforting but strangely renewing. In the experience of dislocation we find ourselves. Deconstruction leads to reconstruction. In the time of exile and spiritual homelessness we rediscover the heart's true home.

We are called to go with Jesus into places of pain or confusion, into areas – literal and metaphorical – that will be at once testing and revelatory. This book can help us reflect on our own discipleship and identify times and seasons in our life where Jesus is wanting to remould and reshape us. Indeed, the experience of prayer itself can be a liminal state, demanding of us that we let go of beliefs or ways of doing things that have got us into a rut, and beckoning us to fresh discoveries of God. In our personal lives and times of prayer we often find ourselves thirsting for something more. The signs that we are ready to embark on a spiritual adventure might begin with a sense of holy listlessness, a certain discontent with our present spiritual life, a holy dissatisfaction and a dawning sense that God is calling us forwards. In this book the concept of liminality becomes a hermeneutical key to look at familiar texts and a lens through which we bring into sharper focus and clarity the transitions to which we are called today in our spiritual journeying.

This journey

In Chapter 1 we will explore the significance of Jesus' coming to the River Jordan. We will reflect on the meaning of the forgotten fact that Jesus not only enters the water, he crosses it. It is truly a threshold of something new. What is happening to Jesus? How does he experience the bereavement and exhilaration of leaving things behind, moving out to a place where he is not known? What does that mean for us who would follow him?

In Chapter 2 we follow Jesus into the marginal lands of the Judean desert. We will discover it to be a place of raw beauty, a wild place where the wind blasts unmercifully at times and a place where, even today, the wild beasts howl. We will see how Jesus experiences exposure and enclosure in the wilderness. In Chapter 3 we venture with Jesus across northern ranges, to the coast of Tyre and Sidon (Mark 7). Leaving behind the comfort zone of 'home', inherited prejudices, stereotypes and complacencies, we will discover new, unsettling and disturbing ways of seeing things, new ways of doing things – an alternative world view, represented in the Greek Syrophoenician woman.

In Chapter 4, with the disciples we quit Capernaum's shoreline of safety, crossing the demon-filled sea to the other side, place of the Gadarene demoniacs. This prompts us to look at our shadow side. Next, in Chapter 5, we reach beyond Samaria's border and join Jesus with the woman at Jacob's Well. We will be stirred to revisit and revise our usual image of God and self.

Chapter 6 summons us to ascend into the hills north of Galilee and join Jesus at prayer atop Mount Hermon. We experience how prayer can be transfiguring for us too.

Then we move to Jerusalem itself. In Chapter 7 we discover its forgotten threshold. In Chapter 8 we join Jesus in his climb towards Jerusalem (John 11), up the Mount of Olives, the eschatological, end-time mount (Zech. 14) and the threshold of the holy city. We join Mary and Martha in the shattering experience of turning inside-out their most cherished doctrines of God and humanity.

Chapter 9 takes us to Jerusalem's garden of struggle, Gethsemane. We trace Christ's movement from resistance and hesitation to submission and acceptance. We ask: What is holding you back? With what are you grappling right now? As the Good Friday event passes into the liminal darkness of Holy Saturday, we ponder the call into paschal prayer, the dark night of the soul, where God is actively at work.

Finally, in Chapter 10 we recall how the risen Christ goes before his disciples into Galilee, and explore how he is waiting to surprise us in liminal places in our own contexts.[5]

Using this book

The book is designed to be used by both individuals and groups. Questions at the end of each chapter are provided to stimulate personal reflection and group discussion. Three readerships are in mind. First, it is for Christians who are longing for movement and progress in their spiritual lives. Second, for those who support others on their spiritual journey – those who serve as spiritual directors, soul-friends or accompaniers. The appendix identifies different models of spiritual direction related to the transitions, and can be used profitably by spiritual directors' supervision or support groups. Liminality may turn out to be a key theme in spiritual direction. Third, the book will be a valuable resource for preachers, with its inclusion of the five Gospel readings for Year A in the Revised Common Lectionary (2014 and so on), widely used across the denominations.[6] For this reason it would also make an ideal resource for Lent: on Sundays churches can look at the relevant Gospel passage and on weekdays remaining chapters can form the heart of a course for parish groups. It is recommended that course participants keep a journal or notebook in which to note and reflect on the transitions taking place in themselves as they undertake this life-changing journey.

1

Wading across the river

'In those days Jesus came from Nazareth of Galilee and was baptized by John in the Jordon.' As always Mark puts it so succinctly (Mark 1.9), but behind these words lies a journey Jesus undertook with mixed feelings.

There was, of course, the outer journey. Jesus left the verdant terrain of the Galilee region and headed southwards down the great rift valley towards the arid desert. Lush green hills were replaced by the stark, sun-breached limestone cliffs. A comfortable and reassuring climate that enjoyed a generous share of rainfall gave way to the testing environment of the Jordan valley, where temperatures reach 45 degrees as the river flows to the lowest point on earth. Jesus was also quitting the traditional, inherited and often parochial views of Nazareth for a region known for its daring apocalyptic expectation: the Essene community of Qumran, only 8 km (5 miles) from the traditional site of the baptism, was super-critical of the Temple regimes and longed for God's imminent intervention in history.

An inner journey was taking place as Jesus undertook this 160 km (100-mile) journey to the Baptist at the Jordan. Exhilaration blended with apprehension. There was no doubt a sense of relief and release as Jesus left his hometown, the village of perhaps 200 souls, where he had spent his first 30 years. Now he was venturing towards something uncertain, exciting, unpredictable, a new mission. No doubt Jesus felt pangs of sadness as he parted from mother, siblings and friends in the village with whom he had shared so many years of childhood, adolescence and young adulthood. He was breaking ties of kith and kin and, as we shall see, gaining an entirely new family. There was the pain of separation in his heart. Literally, he was leaving the familiar behind.

But there was also an overwhelming sense of destiny and vocation. This was a journey he had to make. The call was irresistible; a divine compulsion stirring within him. And with this came a deep sense of surrender to the divine will, symbolized in his plunging into the waters of the Jordan: the submersion bespoke a submission to the summons of God. The Jordan turns out to be a truly liminal space, the threshold of a new beginning. And although Jesus undertakes this journey alone, in the eyes of the biblical writers he is always a corporate, representative figure: the descriptions 'Son of Man', 'suffering servant' and Paul's 'new Adam' all suggest that Jesus is not one solitary figure but stands for all of us – his journey is ours too.

'Jesus came from Nazareth.' These four words encapsulate a range of transitions that Jesus is making. First, as we noted, he is relinquishing ties of family and friends, saying goodbye to long-established relationships. He will find himself saying 'whoever comes to me and does not hate father and mother, wife and children, brothers and sisters, yes, even life itself, cannot be my disciple' (Luke 14.26). He will ask: 'Who are my mother and my brothers?' (Mark 3.33). He is creating a new set of relationships, with the disciples and the women who will be supporting him.

Second, Jesus is shedding expectations and job descriptions that he has grown up with. He has been working as a *tecton* – usually translated 'carpenter', the word denotes craftsman in wood or stone, even a builder. Scholars believe it highly likely that Jesus worked as a builder on the construction site of Sefforis – just 6.5 km (4 miles) north of Nazareth; it was being completely rebuilt at precisely the time Jesus was working. Indeed, Sefforis was the regional capital and was called by Josephus 'the jewel of Galilee'. Jesus is making the transition to a new kind of building task – it is interesting to note how often he uses the imagery of building in his sayings ('on this rock I will build my church', Matt. 16.18; 'a wise man who built his house on rock', Matt. 7.24). He expresses the cost of discipleship in a building metaphor: 'Which of you, intending to build a tower, does not first sit down and estimate the cost, to see whether he has enough to complete it?' (Luke 14.28). In fact his mission can be summed up, like that of Jeremiah (Jer. 1.10), in terms of building and demolition (Matt. 27.40). Jesus is shifting gear. He is starting a new work of construction. He is moving into a new set of priorities. He is now intent on building the reign of God.

Third, this is underpinned by his explorations into new ways of praying. In his years in Nazareth, prayer was based on the synagogue and in the family. There were also the regular annual festivals of the Temple in Jerusalem.[1] Now he is becoming itinerant: 'the Son of Man has nowhere to lay his head' (Luke 9.58). He is becoming a pilgrim and wayfarer, and traditional patterns of prayer will no longer be possible. Jesus will now pray in the hills (Luke 6.12) and in lonely desert-like places (Mark 1.35; 6.30–32). He is moving into a new spiritual experience, a fresh way of encountering God his Father. He is entering upon untried and challenging ways of praying.

Jesus 'was baptized by John in the Jordan'. What is the significance of the Jordan? Why could Jesus not be baptized in the Sea of Galilee, for example? He is positioning himself in precisely the place where the Hebrew people of old entered the Land of Promise: the Jordan is the threshold of Jericho and the very edge of the sacred land. Jesus is placing himself exactly at the point where the exodus journey ended and the tribes entered into their longed-for homeland under Joshua (Josh. 3). Like the Red Sea itself at the start of the exodus story, the Jordan changes from being a barrier to being a crossing-place, locus of fundamental transition. Here the people experienced a profound reshaping of their identity. They had been refugees and slaves, escaping from Pharaoh's tyranny in Egypt. Homeless nomads were becoming residents in a territory they cherished. Scholars consider that the designation 'Hebrew' derives from the concept of the *Habiru*, which denotes an inferior, landless, shifting population, without a name or identity.[2] But at the Jordan nobodies were becoming somebodies. In this passage through the waters of the Jordan, something changed in the soul of the people: they gained a new dignity and a new future; their wilderness wanderings had come to an end; now they were entering upon an entirely new phase of their existence. This experience of profound change anticipates phrases used by the prophet Isaiah:

You shall no more be termed Forsaken,
  and your land shall no more be termed Desolate;
but you shall be called My Delight Is in Her,
  and your land Married.

(Isa. 62.4)

The writer of the first letter of Peter is to echo this language in relation to the Christian vocation: 'you are a chosen race, a royal priesthood, a holy nation, God's own people . . . Once you were not a people, but now you are God's people' (1 Peter 2.9, 10). Jesus is to receive confirmation of his call and identity at this selfsame place of transition: 'a voice came from heaven, "You are my Son, the Beloved; with you I am well pleased"' (Mark 1.11). In the waters of prayer we too can hear the Father's voice and discern our call: 'The voice of the LORD is over the waters; the God of glory thunders, the LORD, over mighty waters' (Ps. 29.3).

Other aspects of the baptism of Christ speak to our transitions. A dove is seen flying over the scene, but this is not the dove of peace – you don't find this idea in the Bible. For Luke, who emphasizes the physicality of the dove ('the Holy Spirit descended upon him in bodily form like a dove' (3.22)), doves mean only one thing: they are birds of sacrifice, whose blood was shed at Jesus' presentation in the Temple as a 40-day infant (Luke 2.24). The dove bespeaks the Holy Spirit but is inseparable from its association with pain and cost.

And so the baptism of Jesus is not the peaceful scene often depicted in Western art and in the religious imagination, such as in Piero della Francesca's masterpiece in London's National Gallery. The iconology of the Byzantine tradition gets closer to the truth, with its flowing waves of water. The baptism was a scary, liminal experience. The heavens were not gently opened up: the Greek text (Mark 1.10) carries the meaning of their being torn open, ripped apart. And the river itself? Today the Jordan at this point is a sluggish, slow-moving meandering stream, reduced to a trickle as 98 per cent of its waters have been diverted for agricultural and domestic use (otherwise they end up unusable in the Dead Sea). But in Joshua's day and at the baptism of Jesus, the Jordan was a dangerous torrent – rapids and waterfalls were found where now it is a brackish stream. Psalm 42.7 refers to the Jordan: 'Deep calls to deep at the thunder of your cataracts; all your waves and your billows have gone over me.' It was a place of risk. Here Jesus prays (Luke 3.21). Here he receives a fresh sense of his identity from heaven itself. Here he decisively leaves behind the culture and mindset of Nazareth and enters on the most risky stage of his life. In his book *Transitions*, William Bridges describes transition as 'a neutral zone'.[3] This was no neutral zone for either Joshua or Jesus: Jesus was plunged into fast-flowing torrents, a zone of hazardous and life-threatening waters. His descent into the waters and re-emergence foreshadow the crucifixion, burial and resurrection.

What we don't normally appreciate is that Jesus does not just enter these swirling threatening waters, he wades across them: he makes a passage through the ferocious eddies and currents. He starts on the east bank at Bethany-beyond-Jordan (John 1.28) and he crosses to the west bank in order to enter the Judean desert. This makes the Jordan truly a *limen*, a threshold. For Jesus it was a place of letting go; in more than one way, an experience of transition. His journey can be ours. Two themes call out.

Vocational change

First, there are the transitions we must make in terms of our vocation and focus. Of course, it begins when we experience the trauma and joy of first leaving home. Later there are times in our life when we again need to break free from our Nazareth and leave behind routines of work or ministry that have become, perhaps, drudgery, a treadmill, fostering stagnation of soul not growth. There are times when a new vocation unfolds or a new set of priorities calls us to change gear radically. The experience of births and deaths can catapult us into the liminal zone, so too can being fired from a job or given a worrying medical diagnosis.

The changes we face in vocational shifts are varied. There is the experience of being deskilled, a letting go of one's past career and one's identity bound up in it, the loss of past confidences, where a sense of vulnerability is acute. There is a sense in which we must face an unmaking and remaking.

There is the pain of bereavement closely associated with this, a sense of dislocation involved where a move is required from familiar ways and cherished communities of support. We may need to let go of ties to the former community where we had a deep sense of belonging. In ordained ministry, the loss of privacy as one moves from being a private citizen to public property and into a representative role can be experienced as a painful bereavement of former freedoms. There can be a loss of self-determination: one is no longer one's own but a servant of the Church. There may be the experience of stress as a diversity of new demands can often be felt as perplexing or even overwhelming.

All these can be carried into prayer – experienced now as a turbulent place, with eddies, whirlpools, rapids and unexpectedly strong currents; a torrent where boulders, other detritus and rubbish get forced along. The river of prayer becomes a place of attrition and erosion, where stones get their corners knocked off. But prayer can at the same time be experienced as a place of profound transformation and creativity, where a new identity is being shaped and formed – waters can break down and build up. Important biblical traditions resonate, helping to make sense of the experience.[4]

Changes in prayer

Second, we may be nudged into new ways of prayer. We may come, with Jesus, from Nazareth, via the deep valley, to the waters of the Jordan. The mystic John of the Cross (1542–91) describes the changes that can take place in prayer through the image of 'dark water'. From his prison in the Toledo city walls, John could hear few sounds but the rushing waters of the River Tajo below.[5] This became an image to communicate the mysterious way in which God flows into human prayer: '*He made darkness and the dark water his hiding place* [Ps. 18:10–11] . . . this darkness . . . and . . . the dark water of his dwelling denote the obscurity of faith in which he is enclosed.'[6] The darkness refers to a process of radical dispossession that John sees at the heart of prayer's movement from egocentricity to God-centredness, a process in which God seeks to reshape us and convert the ego.

John's contemporary, Teresa of Avila (1515–82), uses a different image to describe the changes that can take place in prayer.[7] Teresa develops the patristic concept of the Triple Way, which suggests that the spiritual journey will go through three major phases of purgation/repentance, illumination/receptive prayer towards union. Teresa uses this as a basis to shape the spiritual journey she describes in *The Interior Castle*. Depicting the soul as a crystal castle with many rooms, Christ dwelling at the centre, she invites the reader to trace a journey through successive stages in order to reach a state of mystical union. The image conveys the beauty and potential of the soul; the door to the castle, and indeed its weaving corridor, is the experience of prayer. As Williams observes:

> If the soul is a home for God, it is a home with an enormous abundance of rooms, and we shall need to know where we are if we are not to be deceived and think we have encountered God when we have not . . . the journey inward is a journey to the place where God's love meets and mingles with the life of the soul, and thus we need to keep moving through the rooms until we find the middle of what sounds remarkably like a maze . . . We do not know where the boundaries are if we never move forward and walk into them . . . We need to know what we are capable of, positively and negatively.[8]

Three ways

The adventure of prayer begins with the **Purgative Way** of prayer in the first three rooms of Teresa's interior castle, which represent an increasing detachment from the things of the world and a process of deepening repentance and humility. In the first room of self-knowledge, Teresa cries: 'O souls redeemed by the blood of Jesus Christ! Learn to understand yourselves! . . . The soul's capacity is much greater than we can realize.'[9] The soul must understand both its darkness without Christ's purgation, and its capacity for union with God. In the second room Teresa calls the reader to have 'a very determined determination' – a deep resolve to conquer the pull to turn back to the attractions of the world, in order to remain very focused and single-minded in the interior journey. The third room describes the stability and predictability of respectable routines and normal disciplines of the Christian life, like active discursive meditation. A sign or indicator that the soul is ready to move on from these reveals itself in a holy restlessness or discontent with unfulfilling dutiful praying – a craving for a greater interior freedom and a desire to jump off the treadmill of Christian life. This marks a turning point in the journey and a readiness for transition into the next phase. It is time to learn new ways of praying.

The journey takes a major step forward into the **Illuminative Way** through Teresa's fourth room, a place of new discovery that opens us up to 'supernatural prayer'. Humphreys explains: 'Supernatural prayer is where God takes over. It is also called infused contemplation, passive prayer, mystical prayer, or infused prayer. All labels, again, mean the same thing. This type of prayer means that God is communicating with the person.'[10] Teresa advises: 'if you would progress a long way on this road and ascend to the mansions of your desire, the important thing is not to think much, but to love much; do, then, whatever most arouses you to love.'[11] Here Teresa introduces her readers to 'the Prayer of Quiet' by means of a powerful picture: while active discursive prayer – using many words and images – can be likened to a basin receiving water from lengthy man-made conduits, pipelines and aqueducts of human effort, the Prayer of Quiet is like a basin placed very close to the spring, at its very source, where the water can flow into it unceasingly and without effort: such is the heart of contemplative prayer. The heart becomes enlarged (cf. Ps. 119.32); there is a greater capacity for prayer, a letting go of former restrictive practices of prayer and a movement from the primacy of ego to the initiative of God.

But, says Teresa, there is no need to rest even here. The **Unitive Way** beckons: we may go deeper into God in Teresa's remaining rooms, which explore different dimensions of contemplative prayer. The fifth room is a place of liberation where the soul learns to 'fly' in a new freedom. Using another memorable image, Teresa describes how the soul, like a butterfly emerging from a chrysalis (representing prayers of human effort), leaves behind the silkworm's cocoon, dies to its former way of life and arises metamorphosed into new liberty. 'It has wings now: how it can be content to crawl along slowly when it is able to fly?'[12] But there are new dangers to face: the butterfly soul is vulnerable to increased spiritual conflicts at this stage.

The sixth room opens the pilgrim-soul to the discovery of a glittering treasury in the inner reaches of the castle. The soul is approaching the place where Christ dwells in splendour in the inner room, and it stumbles on his storehouse of breathtaking treasures, which may include extraordinary spiritual experiences: locutions (a sense of a divine 'inner word'), a sense of ecstasy, rapture or unexpected sudden awareness of God's presence within; visions of different kinds; the gift of tears. Teresa insists that all should be tested, and gives clear guidelines for discernment. She is adamant that God should not be sought for these experiences, but for God alone.

However, in these rooms there is also an experience of pain. There are both inner spiritual distresses and external assaults – unfriendly gossip, misunderstanding, rejection and sometimes physical pains too, including illness. As Bielecki puts it:

> Suffering places us in a crucible, and like gold, we emerge refined, purified and strengthened . . . The meaning of suffering is summed up in the mystery of the cross: Teresa believed that the cross is the gift God gives to his intimate friends.[13]

In the sixth room Teresa speaks of the soul's betrothal to God, while in the seventh she uses the daring language of mystical marriage to describe union with God as an abiding awareness and permanent consciousness of unity with the indwelling Christ. But this is not at the cost of total withdrawal from the world: Teresa recalls the story of Martha and Mary to call for an integration between action and contemplation: 'This I should like us to attain: we should desire and engage in prayer, not for our enjoyment, but for the sake of acquiring this strength which fits us for service.'[14]

We must not see rigidity of thought regarding successive stages in a spiritual journey where there is, in fact, fluidity. Teresa is clear: 'You mustn't think of these dwelling places in such a way that each of you would follow in file after the other.'[15] In another place she writes: 'this castle has, as I said, many dwelling places: some up above, others down below, others to the sides ...'[16] Teresa provides a map or a sketch of the spiritual life. The main point is: whatever room of prayer you find yourself in, this room has a door facing you right now, beckoning you to yet-unexplored reaches of prayer. Don't get stuck in one room – go on, try the next door, see where it leads! Or to return to the image of the river, do not stay stranded on the bank – dare to enter the risky waters.

Return to the waters

Baptism is not a one-off event in the lives of Christians, rather it sets the pattern for the whole of the Christian life. We pass through the baptismal waters as the first crossing of our Jordan but we are called to be a pilgrim people through all of life. Each Easter Christians revisit their baptism and remind themselves that they are called from death to life. As the baptismal liturgy puts it:

> Through the deep waters of death you brought your Son, and raised him to life in triumph ... We thank you, Father, for the water of Baptism: in it we are buried with Christ in his death. By it we share in his resurrection. Through it we are reborn by the Holy Spirit.[17]

But all through the year God is calling us to step into the swirling waters, to wade into the deep, to drown our small ideas, let go of certain dreams or sins, to submerge our narrowed hopes or worn-out practices and to hear again the call of Christ. We emerge, dripping like Jesus, to face a new future. We are a baptismal people, a river people, who know the Jordan in our daily experience. We are a people ready to make transitions, in the ways we pray and in the ways we serve. As John Henry Newman put it:

For in truth we are not called once only, but many times; all through our life Christ is calling us. He called us first in Baptism; but afterwards also; whether we obey his voice or not, He graciously calls us still . . . He calls us on from grace to grace, and from holiness to holiness, while life is given us . . . we are all in the course of calling, on and on, from one thing to another, having no resting place, but mounting towards our eternal rest, and obeying one command only to have another put upon us.[18]

Questions for reflection

1 How far can you identify with Jesus wading through the waters from the east bank to the west? What is your Nazareth, and where is your river of transition? Do you need to break out of a spiritual routine that has become an unproductive rut or a constriction of your soul?

2 In what ways can you see prayer as being like a river? What associations or biblical references does this evoke for you?

3 What is your heart telling you about the transitions you are currently experiencing?

4 What room of prayer do you find yourself in, according to Teresa's map of the journey? What is the next door facing you calling you to? Will you open it?

5 Is there anything or any relationship in your life that you need to relinquish, to enable you to move forward and embrace the future? Is there a 'No' you need to say that will enable a bigger and more courageous 'Yes'?

Prayer exercise

Recall a recent transition/shift/movement in your life of discipleship/prayer journey. Bring it back to life in your memory and senses. How did you feel about it then, when it took place? Did any Scripture or experience of Jesus resonate with it? How do you feel about it now? What is God saying to you in this transition?

Or

On a fresh piece of paper draw a personal timeline to recall the transitions you have faced. Draw a horizontal line and mark it into the decades of your life. Above the line note major events and transitions, including new jobs, house-moves, births and deaths, new ministries. Below the line try to note how you felt at these moments of change. How did you experience God at these moments when, as it were, you waded across the turbulent river? If in a group setting, you might like to reflect on this with a partner. Bring this to a close by giving thanks for God's providence in your life, and entrust your future to him. Conclude by reading aloud Isaiah 43.1–2: 'Do not fear, for I have redeemed you; I have called you by name, you are mine. When you pass through the waters, I will be with you.'

For further reading

W. Bridges, *Transitions: Making Sense of Life's Changes* (Cambridge, MA: Da Capo Press, 2004).

J. Hagberg and R. A. Guelich, *The Critical Journey: Stages in the Life of Faith* (Sheffield: Sheffield Publishing Company, 1995).

D. W. Judy, *Discerning Life Transitions: Listening Together in Spiritual Direction* (New York: Morehouse Publishing, 2010).

G. O'Collins, *Second Journey: Spiritual Awareness and the Mid-Life Crisis* (Leominster: Gracewing, 1995).

P. Shaw, *Finding Your Future: The Second Time Around* (London: Darton, Longman & Todd, 2006).

2

Advancing through desert margins

The desert is the archetypal liminal place. It is the space between the river and the city. Jesus not only enters the desert himself, he also leads his disciples through it, notably on his final journey to the holy city. There is no other way between Jericho and Jerusalem but by way of the desert. Then it was a liminal place as the threshold of his passion: a letting go of his ministry of healing and teaching and an entering into a new phase. But earlier, Jesus is driven to the desert by the Spirit after his baptism in the river. This is a transitional moment for Jesus. The 40 days' sojourn echoes vividly the 40 years' trek through the desert made by the Israelites in their search for freedom. Now Jesus enters the rocky canyons of the Judean wilderness. The desert is a raw, wild, untamed place, calling forth authenticity and honesty from the soul. It is an eroded place, where the elements of wind and sun and water split rocks and crumble cliffs, symbolizing the brokenness of humanity. It is an open place, bespeaking of the vulnerability of the soul. And yet it is an awesomely beautiful and inspiring place, reflecting the potentialities of the human spirit.

Mark puts it succinctly: 'And the Spirit immediately drove him out into the wilderness. He was in the wilderness for forty days, tempted by Satan; and he was with the wild beasts; and the angels waited on him' (1.12). For Jesus the desert turns out to be a place of wild beasts where he encounters jackal and hyena. There are scorpions underfoot. He is exposed to the elements – to howling wind and unforgiving, blazing sun. But he is exposed to other dangers too – he must grapple with powerful temptations and struggle with demons. Peter wrote: 'Like a roaring lion your adversary the devil prowls around, looking for someone to devour' (1 Peter 5.8). As the parable of the Good Samaritan reminds us, the desert is also the place of bandits and terrorists – a risky place in every sense. And yet Jesus is also enfolded in the care of angels and discerns the Father's voice. The desert terrain is a powerful symbol of Christian prayer and the transitions we are invited to make. There seems to be, in Jesus' experience and in ours, a double movement: increasing exposure and deepening enclosure.

The desert invites us to consider our image of self – who we think we are. How do you see yourself? We need to hold two things in tension: like Jesus himself we are exposed to the reality of our vulnerability and human fragility, exposed to temptation and to distorting visions of reality (Matt. 4.1–11); but we are also, like Jesus, enfolded in the enveloping truth that we are beloved, God's child. In this chapter we will look at these two movements of prayer as they reveal themselves in the experience of Jesus, the desert fathers and in our lives too.

Expanding exposure: the place of vulnerability

Jesus in the desert experiences his humanity. He thirsts and hungers. He exposes himself to the wiles of the enemy. The threefold temptation to power, prestige and pride is a threefold journey, and on each occasion Jesus teeters at the very edge. First, he is taken to the dried up and scorched river bed, littered by boulders and rocks washed down in the winter storms and flash floods. At the edge of hunger, the limit of human endurance, he is tempted to turn stones into bread. Second, he is taken to the pinnacle of the Temple, the very brink of the Temple area towering over the Kidron valley. There he is invited to the suicidal act of throwing himself down. Third, he is taken to 'a very high mountain' (Matt. 4.8). The devil shows him all the kingdoms of the world: 'All these I will give you, if you will fall down and worship me' (v. 9). Each of these 'edges' could have been a terminus, literally 'a dead end', but Jesus transforms them into liminal spaces that usher him into a fresh discovery of the power of God's word.

In conquering these temptations Jesus is experiencing a radical relearning, for the attitudes behind them were precisely the prevailing values he had probably encountered daily in his labouring at Sefforis. There, the very buildings going up – opulent villas for the exploitative urban elite – symbolized in stone a craving for power and prestige. Now he decisively rejects these. Jesus faces up to the reality of human nature – he sees the human potential for following distorted visions of reality, false dreams, the perversion of our powers. As the Letter to the Hebrews puts it: 'he had to become like his brothers and sisters in every respect . . . Because he himself was tested by what he suffered, he is able to help those who are being tested' (Heb. 2.17–18). The desert landscape spoke to him of what is real in the human condition. The burning bright intensity of the sun shows up places of light and shade, and the shade is so tempting. Jesus saw vividly and dramatically the choices open to everyone: the risk of staying out in the sun, and the seductive shadows. 'Although he was a Son, he learned obedience through what he suffered' (Heb. 5.8). His sojourn in the desert shows Jesus' radical solidarity with us in our desert places.

But it also taught him about the human longing for the divine Spirit. Physicality pointed to spirituality: the arid wastelands became a picture of the human soul. Jesus, who loved the prophet Isaiah (quoting Isaiah 61 in Luke 4 and alluding to Isaiah's Servant Songs), surely recalled God's promise: 'I will pour water on the thirsty land, and streams on the dry ground. I will pour out my spirit' (Isa. 44.3); 'When the poor and needy seek water and there is none, and their tongue is parched with thirst . . . I will open rivers on the bare heights, and fountains in the midst of the valleys' (Isa. 41.17–18). If Jesus saw, in his exposure in the desert, humanity's potentiality for evil and wrong choices, he also saw the human capacity for the divine Spirit, mirrored so powerfully in the barren longing terrain. The desert speaks powerfully of humanity's spiritual poverty and thirst. As the desert father Macarius wrote in the fourth century: 'We have an insatiable longing for the Spirit, to shine out – the more spiritual gifts we enjoy, the more insatiable is the heavenly desire in our hearts, the more hungry and thirsty we are for more grace.'[1]

The desert is a powerful symbol of Christian prayer because it is a place of truth, of radical, searing honesty. There is no place for pretence, for role-playing, for the wearing of masks before

God. The sun burns into the soul. Here we come out into the open, are exposed to elements human and physical – this is a place of spiritual nakedness. Jerome said: 'the desert strips you bare'. Here prayer gets real. Our self-protective barriers and defences must crumble before God. The false, competitive self must die; the self or ego identified with our persona (Greek – mask) that we present to the world must wither and fade away. The image of ourselves that we like others to see – confident, competent – is often shaped or conditioned by our culture, by advertisements, by the modern preoccupation with 'image' or cult of celebrity, by the compulsions and illusions of our age. People like a good performance; want to see beautiful bodies, well dressed, unwrinkled, attractive; admire the ones who seem to be wealthy and successful. They worship images of perfection. This is a self-image or image of the self that we would like to project to others – we think that our worth, our value, comes from what other people say about us, how they acclaim us and appreciate us. But this is the illusory self, clamouring for attention – a wax mask that must melt in the heat of the desert.

The desert fathers and mothers went into the desert to discover God; in the process they discovered themselves too. Seekers came to request a word of counsel and advice – 'Give me a word, father.' Often the word offered penetrates all pretences and role-playing, slices through masks and artificialities and cuts to the quick, exposing falsities. In the desert the fathers recognize demons and angels. In the dazzling light of the day they are ready to expose human foibles and self-importances.

> One day when Abba John was sitting in front of the church, the brethren were consulting him about their thoughts. One of the old men who saw it became a prey to jealousy and said to him, 'John, your vessel is full of poison.' Abba John said to him, 'That is very true, abba; and you have said that when you only see the outside, but if you were able to see the inside, too, what would you say then?'[2]

Here the passions and lusts, fantasies and temptations are magnified and seen in all their ferocity as undermining true identity in

God. Anthony the Great said: 'He who wishes to live in solitude in the desert is delivered from three conflicts: hearing, speech, and sight; there is only one conflict for him and that is with fornication.'[3]

We must come to terms with our weaknesses. Maybe the angels and demons are within us – not external entities but interior aspects of our soul. The desert fathers sometimes overestimated their capabilities:

> Abba John said to his older brother: 'I should like to be free of all care, like the angels, who do not work but ceaselessly offer worship to God.' So he took off his cloak and went away into the desert. After a week, he came back to his brother. When he knocked on the door, he heard his brother say, before he opened it, 'Who are you?' He said, 'I am John, your brother.' But he replied, 'John has become an angel, and henceforth he is no longer among men.'

Finally, opening the door to him the next day, the elder brother said to him, 'You are a man and must once again work in order to eat.' Then John made a prostration before him, saying, 'Forgive me.'[4]

Abba Ammoes reveals the paradox. He appeared to his colleagues sometimes like an angel, sometimes like Satan:

> At first, Abba Ammoes said to Abba Isaiah, 'What do you think of me now?' He said to him, 'You are an angel, Father.' Later on he said to him, 'And now what do you think of me?' He replied, 'You are like Satan. Even when you say a good word to me, it is like steel.'[5]

So the first spiritual movement in the desert of prayer is towards increasing exposure – to the reality of sin and temptation, to the reality of the self and above all to God's Spirit. This is symbolized very powerfully in the winds that race across the Judean desert. The desert is a breezy place, and the different winds illustrate the different workings of the Spirit in our life. There is the cooling afternoon breeze that blows in from the Mediterranean. This brings refreshment to those struggling in the blazing desert heat, bespeaking the Holy Spirit the Comforter, the one who renews the weary.

A second wind speaks of the Holy Spirit the discomforter. The Hamseen wind is a hot, dry scorching wind that originates from the deserts of the south. It is thick and desiccating and marked by dust-clouds. The Holy Spirit can be a disturbing and unsettling presence in our lives. If we find ourselves complacent, settled or stuck in our praying, then we need such a Spirit and such a wind to move us on, somehow, in our spiritual life. A third wind that blows across the Judean desert is the stormy winter wind. For most of the year the desert is a parched, baked landscape where grasses turn brown, burnt in the sun. Then, unexpectedly, come the winter winds and their generous gift of rain. When there is a downpour on the Mount of Olives, the water runs eastwards towards the great rift valley and flash floods sweep through the desert ravines, shifting boulders and cutting the edges of the valley. When the wet wind blows on the desert it is very welcome indeed – it is the harbinger of spring, turning back the drought and enabling new shoots and fresh growth of plants, the miraculous spreading out of a green mantle across the desert. This speaks to us of the Holy Spirit who comes to re-energize us, awakening us into new life. We may not predict the moving of the wind in our spiritual lives but we must expose ourselves to its presence: 'the wind blows where it chooses, and you hear the sound of it, but you do not know where it comes from or where it goes. So it is with everyone who is born of the Spirit' (John 3.8).

Deepening enclosure: the place of affirmation

High above the oasis city of Jericho, clinging barnacle-like to the towering cliff face, is the Monastery of the Temptation. It incorporates a remarkable cave where traditionally Jesus hid himself in his 40-day stay in the wilderness. It is certain that Jesus entered a cave to pray, as they are plentiful and inviting spaces of cool – caves are a characteristic feature of Judean monasticism to this day.

Jesus enters his desert-cave with these words ringing in his ears: 'You are my Son, the Beloved; with you I am well pleased' (Mark 1.11). This is the experience of enclosure: the embrace of

God in the depths of the earth and in the depths of prayer. It is the place of intimacy with God. In the darkness of the cave, Jesus allows himself to be held in the arms of his Father, taking deep with him the awesome affirmation made at his baptism. In his desert prayer he is to explore the meaning of this.

The desert fathers and mothers prayed in caves. Every monastic settlement in the Judean desert consisted of caves – a few are spacious, with a chapel area, sleeping and cooking area, but most are small, with just a ledge for a bed. The characteristic teaching of the desert fathers is summed up in this famous saying: 'Go, sit in your cell and your cell will teach you everything.'[6] As Jesus said, 'whenever you pray, go into your room and shut the door and pray to your Father who is in secret; and your Father who sees in secret will reward you' (Matt. 6.6). In these caves one experiences a kind of deafening silence, the sort of silence that rings in your ears. There is a deep sense of being held by God, encompassed, enveloped, reassured. You are 'accepted in the beloved' (Eph. 1.6, AV).

The one who is considered the first ever monk experienced this powerfully. St Anthony's Cave in Egypt is hidden away in Mount Colzim, in a valley that runs down to the Red Sea. It is high up in the cliff face, more than 600 m (2,000 feet) above sea level; the pilgrim can access it today by climbing up many steps. From the cliff face you enter a dark, narrow tunnel more than 6 m (20 feet) in length that finally reaches a chamber in pitch blackness. Inside there is a real sense of enclosure, of being held by God. It does not feel claustrophobic but it does feel that you are in a deep mysterious place concealed from the world and from the blazing sunlight of the desert, wrapped around with the walls of living rock.

A striking feature of the *Letters of St Anthony* is the teaching about *gnosis*, self-knowledge. As Rubenson points out: 'Without knowledge of himself, or, as Anthony says, of his own *spiritual essence*, a man [sic] cannot know God, he cannot understand God's acts of salvation, but by fully understanding himself a man knows his time.'[7] Anthony's *Letters* celebrate a spiritual anthropology:

A sensible man who has prepared himself to be freed at the coming of Jesus knows himself in his spiritual essence, for he who knows himself also knows the dispensations of his Creator, and what he does for his creatures.[8]

Fusing Platonic, Origenist and biblical ideas, Anthony teaches that humanity's 'spiritual essence' consists in being rational; that is, in our capacity for true knowledge of God. His advice is 'know thyself'.

Thomas Merton observes that at the heart of what the desert fathers and mothers are saying is the experience of the 'emergence of the true secret self':

What the Fathers sought most of all was their own true self, in Christ. And in order to do this, they had to reject completely the false, formal self, fabricated under social compulsion in 'the world.' A life of work and prayer enabled the old superficial self to be purged away and permitted the gradual emergence of the true, secret self in which the Believer and Christ were 'one spirit.'[9]

The cave of prayer becomes both a tomb and a womb: a place where the old illusory ego learns to die and where the new self in Christ is born; a liminal place of undoing and remaking, of death and resurrection. As Henri Nouwen puts it:

Solitude is not a private therapeutic place. Rather, it is the place of conversion, the place where the old self dies and the new self is born . . . Solitude is the place where Christ remodels us in his own image and frees us from the victimizing compulsions of the world. Solitude is the place of our salvation.[10]

In the cave of prayer the life is 'hidden with Christ in God' (Col. 3.3). What other people think is not the issue. Amma Sarah said, 'If I prayed God that all people should approve of my conduct, I should find myself a penitent at the door of each one, but I shall rather pray that my heart may be pure toward all.'[11] Amma Syncletica speaks a word of wisdom that resonates with the lure of today's celebrity culture:

Just as a treasure that is exposed loses its value, so a virtue which is known vanishes; just as wax melts when it is near fire, so the soul is destroyed by praise and loses all the results of its labour. Just as it is impossible to be at the same time both a plant and a seed, so it is impossible for us to be surrounded by worldly honour and at the same time to bear heavenly fruit.[12]

Abba John puts it round the other way: 'even if we are entirely despised in the eyes of men, let us rejoice that we are honoured in the sight of God'.[13] In the cave of prayer, in the experience of deepening enclosure by God, one knows deeply the affirming love of God. And here too we learn the soul's true potential:

Abba Lot went to see Abba Joseph and said to him, 'Abba, as far as I can I say my little office, I fast a little, I pray and meditate, I live in peace and as far as I can, I purify my thoughts. What else can I do?' Then the old man stood up and stretched his hands towards heaven. His fingers became like ten lamps of fire and he said to him, 'If you will, you can become all flame.'[14]

Our potential and vocation is to be ignited by the Spirit, engulfed with his fire, radiant and ablaze with the Spirit himself, the divine flame. Abba Joseph had moments when he could fulfil this potential. There were other times when he struggled with his passions and felt the flame extinguished:

Some brothers happened one day to meet at Abba Joseph's cell. While they were sitting there, questioning him, he became cheerful and, filled with happiness he said to them, 'I am a king today, for I reign over the passions.'[15]

We have to return again and again to the deep reality of who we truly are in Christ. As Abba Isidore put it: 'in obeying the truth, man [sic] surpasses everything else, for he is the image and likeness of God'.[16]

This experience of enclosure resonates with Elijah's story. He had been fleeing many stressful situations; finally he enters a cave at Horeb. A violent storm passes by. Elijah stands in the cleft of the rock; there he encounters God and rediscovers himself.

> Now there was a great wind, so strong that it was splitting mountains and breaking rocks in pieces before the LORD, but the LORD was not in the wind; and after the wind an earthquake, but the LORD was not in the earthquake; and after the earthquake a fire, but the LORD was not in the fire; and after the fire a sound of sheer silence.　　(1 Kings 19.11–12)

The psalms celebrate this reality of being held by God – 'You are a hiding-place', declares Psalm 32.7. 'But I have calmed and quieted my soul, like a weaned child with its mother; my soul is like the weaned child that is with me' (Ps. 131.2). The paradox is that the place of enclosure is a spacious area, expansive, that enlarges the heart, opening up an inner space for God, a cave of the heart.

Questions for reflection

1　What is holding you back from utter exposure to God? Name your barriers, fears, hesitations.
2　What is your experience of being held by God? What feelings or effects on you did it produce?
3　'The most courageous thing we will ever do is to bear humbly the mystery of our own reality.'[17] What do you make of this?
4　How do you find yourself responding to the prayer, attributed to Macrina Wiederkehr: 'God, help me to believe the truth about myself, no matter how beautiful it may be'? Respond with both your head and your heart.
5　Why is a wholesome self-image essential to spiritual progress? What can we do to support those whose self-image is damaged or dented?

Prayer exercise

This is a way of practising a prayer that is first extravert in character, then introvert. Begin by opening your arms wide. Let this bespeak utter exposure to God – open yourself to the wind of God's Spirit. Stay in this mode as long as you can. What does it feel like? What is God saying to you? Then close your arms around your chest – let this speak to you of the second movement of the desert, enclosure; being held by God. Feel enfolded and hemmed in by God's unconditional love. Permit yourself to be overwhelmed by God. Rest in this experience, as Jesus rested in the cave.

For further reading

B. C. Lane, *The Solace of Fierce Landscapes* (Oxford: Oxford University Press, 2007).

A. Louth, *The Wilderness of God* (London: Darton, Longman & Todd, 2003).

H. J. M. Nouwen, *The Way of the Heart* (London: Darton, Longman & Todd, 1981).

3

Venturing to the coastlands

'Sing to the LORD a new song, his praise from the end of the earth! Let the sea roar and all that fills it, the coastlands and their inhabitants' (Isa. 42.10). Jesus takes his disciples to the brink of the known world, to the very edge of the continent.

He takes them 'off the map' and well beyond the periphery of the historic territory of Israel, the homeland of the disciples, and into the far reaches of the Roman province of Syria. They make a determined trek of perhaps 160 km (100 miles) across the deeply forested hills and mountains north of the Sea of Galilee – a difficult terrain with steeply sided ravines and valleys. Across these borderlands – and in more than one sense – Jesus takes them on a hazardous and exhausting journey they have never trod before, to a place they have never seen. He takes them to the very coast, to the Mediterranean Sea – to present-day Lebanon.

Sidon was a great seaport with a distinguished history. Tyre was noted for its magnificent harbour. Both looked out across the sea to the west. They were significant points of entry for visitors from Greece and Europe, open to a diversity of cultures and traditions as travellers arrived, bringing with them their customs and perspectives. As great ports and trading centres they were the meeting point of ethnicities. Why was Jesus so determined to lead his disciples to this territory, far away from their hometowns? At this coastland he wanted to expose them to new vistas, broader horizons, different ways of doing things. He wanted to provoke a breakthrough to fresh ways of seeing things and trigger an expansive vision. As they stand on the breezy Mediterranean coast lashed by waves, the wind blowing in their faces, they are brought into contact with a wider world, a world they hardly imagined.

In this chapter we recall the episode narrated in Matthew (15.21–27) and Mark (7.24–30). You might like to look up these passages now. Commentators have often found them disturbing or embarrassing, and there are two ways of interpreting the event that transpires. In one reading Jesus is training his disciples to view the world differently. In the alternative reading Jesus himself revises his views, changes his mind and even does a U-turn in his basic attitudes.

In the region of Tyre and Sidon, Jesus encounters a woman described by Mark (7.26) as 'Gentile, of Syrophoenician origin'; Matthew (15.22) calls her a 'Canaanite'. She is a member of an ancient and noble people, a proud maritime community noted for its rich heritage and successful trading and seafaring. Jesus needs to speak to her in the Greek tongue, in contrast to the Aramaic he normally uses. The woman begs Jesus to deliver her daughter from an unclean spirit but Jesus seems to respond negatively: 'Let the children be fed first, for it is not fair to take the children's food and throw it to the dogs' (Mark 7.27). This seems to be a derogatory and harsh response, heightening the priority of the Jewish people and calling Gentiles 'unclean dogs'. The woman responds: 'Sir, even the dogs under the table eat the children's crumbs' (v. 28). Recognizing her humility and faith, Jesus declares that her daughter is freed from the demon.

Matthew, in his account, stresses that it is the disciples who have the problem: 'his disciples came and urged him, saying, "Send her away, for she keeps shouting after us"' (Matt. 15.23). Matthew, too, emphasizes the woman's faith: 'Woman, great is your faith! Let it be done for you as you wish' (v. 28). In the perspective of the first Gospel, Jesus is instructing and teaching his disciples about attitudes to non-Jews: the disciples are the ones who need to change their minds. But Mark's Gospel does not soften the account in this way: it is Jesus himself who appears to change his attitude and move from a standpoint of rejection in relation to what the woman represents, to one of acceptance.

Wherever the shift is to be located, there is a certain playfulness, good humour and even teasing in this encounter. The woman helps to open up a new paradigm by her quick and quirky response; there is laughter in the air. This is an exploration of another's thought-world. Jesus has crossed many barriers to get to this point: he has traversed the physical barrier of the high hills of northern Galilee; made himself an exile by quitting the homeland and entering pagan territory – he is the foreigner, not the woman; crossed a gender barrier in talking to the woman at all; scaled a racial barrier in this encounter with the Syrophoenician; bridged a cultural gap by entering the Greek-speaking Gentile world.

Overcoming duality

Jesus has plunged himself into a different world and taken his disciples with him. He has exposed them to a different way of seeing things that radically turns upside down their former convictions, expressed in John's maxim, 'salvation is from the Jews' (John 4.22). This is a seismic shift, an overturning of models, a breaking of conventions. Jesus was determined to penetrate this world and was prepared, it seems, to change himself. He represents – perhaps to teach his disciples – a dualistic viewpoint. Children and dogs are, as it were, pitted against each other. This seems to represent an either/or view of things, an 'us and them' mentality. But the woman argues for a both/and view: 'even the dogs under the table eat the children's crumbs'. She glimpses the unity of all creation, not the superiority or divine preference or election of one people over against the others. Her vision is all-encompassing; she has crossed the divides in her thinking – dogs and children both belong in God's kingdom; both have needs to be honoured. It seems that in his encounter near Tyre and Sidon, Jesus is taking a controversial stance with the woman for the purposes of polemic and instruction. He heightens the drama to make a point.[1]

The encounter with the woman had a far-reaching impact. It was a link in the chain that enables Gentiles to be Christians today. At the end of Matthew's Gospel the one who said to her, 'I was sent only to the lost sheep of the house of Israel' (15.24) now says: 'Go therefore and make disciples of all nations' (28.19). In Mark's Gospel the one who had said 'it is not fair to take the children's food and throw it to the dogs' (7.27) now says, 'Go into all the world and proclaim the good news to the whole creation' (16.15). For Jesus, the encounter with the other world represented in the person of the Syrophoenician woman was life-changing. He celebrates faraway pagan Tyre and Sidon as a place where mercy will be more likely to be received than in the Jewish towns of Chorazin or Bethsaida on the Sea of Galilee: 'I tell you, on the day of judgement it will be more tolerable for Tyre and Sidon than for you' (Matt. 11.20–22).

In Mark's perspective Jesus had already announced his intention to revolutionize and radically shake up people's thinking. 'The time is fulfilled, and the kingdom of God has come near; repent, and believe in the good news' (1.15). Mark's Gospel gives us these dramatic words as the starting point, the opening lines of Jesus' proclamation. Jesus' call to us is 'repent'. We usually read this in a moralistic way, calling us to penitence, but as recent writers have reminded us, it is a summons to an utterly different way of seeing reality.[2] The word is literally *meta*, meaning 'beyond' or 'large', and *noia*, which translates as 'mind'. Jesus is calling us to 'go beyond the mind' or 'go into the big mind'. He is inviting us to a fresh way of seeing things, a new consciousness. He is demanding that we let go of our former defensive dualistic paradigms and make the transition into a new vision of things that is summed up in the metaphor of the 'kingdom of God'.

Jesus conquers dichotomy

Jesus goes on to teach and practise a gospel that radically embraces all. He crosses boundaries and breaks down barriers. For him, the model of true greatness is the child in the midst (Mark 9.36). The presence of women is welcomed by Jesus (Luke 8.3; 23.49) and he reaches out to those marginalized by society, embracing the leper (Luke 17.10–19). The most significant sign of his all-embracing kingdom, where barriers are overturned, is the meal where Jesus eats with tax collectors and sinners (Luke 5.29–32; 14.12–24). For Jesus, the open table – where everyone, regardless of shame or status, has a treasured place – expresses his readiness to smash barriers and social taboos. Jesus overcomes centuries-long social dichotomies between the 'haves and haves not'.[3]

This culminates in his teaching at the Last Supper and his prayer on the eve of his passion as reflected on in John's Gospel. In the fourth Gospel Jesus talks about 'those who abide in me and I in them' (15.5). In his great prayer of John 17 Jesus pleads: 'that they may all be one. As you, Father, are in me and I am in you, may they also be in us' (17.21). Jesus wants to overcome the divide. This is a radically alternative way of looking at things: to uncover and reveal the unity of creation with God. Jesus' longing culminates in the cross where he is crucified on a structure that sums up his healing of dichotomy: the vertical, transcendent, Godward shaft of the cross meets the horizontal, inclusive arm. Outstretched arms embrace all. The Letter to the Ephesians celebrates how here Jew and Gentile are brought together:

> in his flesh he has made both groups into one and has broken down the dividing wall . . . that he might create in himself one new humanity in place of the two, thus making peace . . . through the cross. (Eph. 2.14–16)

As the Franciscan theologian and later saint Bonaventure observed in the thirteenth century, apparent opposites are united in an unexpected encounter on the cross: darkness meets light, death is vanquished by life and the brokenness of the world is healed as Christ cries out 'it is finished' (John 19.30).[4]

Spirituality and unity

Sadly, Christian spirituality had become infected with divisive, dualistic thinking since the early centuries embraced Platonic thought. This gave rise to disastrous polarities in Christian think-ing as things were pitched against one another: heaven was opposed to earth; the body to the spirit; politics and prayer were to be kept separate. Sacred and secular were delineated with barriers as if they were two separate realms, holy and unholy. The Church and the world are set against each other. There is a natural human tendency towards polarization, keeping things apart – it has to do with being in control, trying to make sense of things neatly, seeing things in black and white – but as we know, it can lead to fundamentalism, racism, homophobia, fear of the other. We feel safer when we oppose, judge, differentiate, label and compare.

We live in a polarized word: Republican vs Democrat, Conservative vs Labour, Protestant vs Catholic, East vs West. Things are often said to be black or white. In the UK, Parliament is based on government and opposition locked in perpetual combat. We are uneasy with the idea of coalition and say, 'It shouldn't be like this. It will never work!' Bifurcation is the preferred option. It has been said that we live in a 'tit for tat universe'.[5] Tragically, we see such duality played out in the Holy Land itself. Two ancient and noble peoples are pitted against each other because of views of the land that are mutually exclusive. The painful divides in the Holy Land today, including the segregation wall or separation barrier aiming to keep apart Palestinian and Jew, are symbolic, poignant and telling. The land that is deemed sacred, that bears the 'footprints of God', the soil that witnessed the revelation of God, is carved up and fragmented. But do we do this, also, to the holy land of prayer?

In spirituality, dualistic thinking has created unnecessary distances and opened up uncalled-for chasms. Where God is thought of as something 'out there' or 'up there', he is seen as remote and unapproachable. But Christian spirituality celebrates the God within, and the breakthrough to non-dualistic thinking comes precisely when the prayer of contemplation is allowed to dissolve the divides between humans and God. It is the entry into a different way of knowing, an alternative way of perceiving reality. Prayer might begin with a sense of God beyond – 'Our Father who art in heaven' – but it dares to pray 'thy kingdom come' and moves to an awareness of the God within: 'Thy will be done on earth as it is in heaven.' It feels OK and non-threatening to conceive of God 'up there' and at a safe distance; it is scary to think of the God within – like Peter, we instinctively say, 'Leave me, Lord! I'm a sinful person!'[6] We need to come to a point where we can say with St Patrick, 'Christ above me, Christ below me, Christ within me.' This is a liminal experience because it requires a letting go, an unlearning (of the idea of 'God up there'), a struggle to come to terms with this before one enters the deeper level of awareness.

The challenge

What is entailed in the transition here, as we meet with different world views? First we must be prepared to move. Jesus undertook an exhausting journey across the northern Galilee hills. We must move, physically or spirituality, in order to seek out the Other, and in the process of relating we discover that the Other is really part of us. The journey towards the Other becomes the discovery that we are all part of one another. The dualisms that had fenced us off, kept us safely apart, dissolve into the astonishing revelation that we belong to each other – I am incomplete without my neighbour. For this transition to take place we must be prepared to lower our self-protective barriers and be ready to be startled or disturbed and shaken out of the comfortable patterns of thinking we're accustomed to. Above all, we should be ready to change, daring to see things from an alternative point of view.

The Syrophoenician woman – we never learn her name – teaches us that unexpected sources can not only instruct us, they can also be life-transformative and revolutionize our understanding of God's ways. Unexplored territories of prayer now beckon us. We are prompted to engage with spiritual writers who may act as a stimulus to fresh ways of praying, as a catalyst to attempt different ways of discovering God and the Scriptures. Such writers or figures may be literally foreign to us and, like the Syrophoenician woman, may have the capacity to subvert our thinking, disrupt our cherished patterns of prayer or interrupt our fixated trains of thought. This is the challenge of the liminal places: we need to be ready to be unnerved, unsettled and spurred on in our spiritual journey; ready for our existing and inherited mindsets to be challenged; able to become explorers once again. As we explore different directions we shall see that the theme of discovering a non-dualistic outlook recurs in quite diverse settings.

Venture east

The location of the Syrophoenician woman suggests that we might begin our explorations with the rich heritage of the Syriac spiritual tradition. St Ephrem (d.373), poet, hymn writer and deacon, represents an outstanding example. Indeed, he acknowledges a personal indebtedness to the story of the Syrophoenician woman, for he concludes many of his poems with allusions to 'the children's crumbs' (Mark 7.28) to end on a note of faith and humility. His great *Hymn on Faith* shows us how he uses powerful imagery and metaphors in his description of the spiritual life:

> See, Fire and Spirit are in the womb of her who bore
>   You;
> See, Fire and Spirit are in the river in which You were
>   baptized.
> Fire and Spirit are in our baptismal font,
> In the Bread and the Cup are Fire and Holy Spirit.

In this poem Ephrem celebrates the mysterious working of the Holy Spirit in the Eucharist and in the spiritual life. Echoing the story of the Syrophoenician woman, he writes:

> Look, Lord, my lap is now filled with the crumbs from
>   Your table
> there is no more room in the folds of my garment,
> So hold back your gift as I worship before You,
> Keep it in Your treasure house in readiness to give
> it us on another occasion.[7]

There certainly are 'other occasions' – for Ephrem was a prolific and inspiring writer. He encourages us to see reality differently, using his famed image of the 'luminous eye' that can look into the hiddenness of God's mystery:

> Blessed is the person who has acquired a luminous eye
> With which he will see how much the angels stand in
>   awe of You, Lord,
> And how audacious is man.[8]

31

Ephrem encourages us to pray for the gift of the inner eye, which penetrates the deep things of God and gives true insight. In this way our prayer can become luminous, radiant and light-revealing:

> Let our prayer be a mirror, Lord, placed before Your
>   face;
> Then Your fair beauty will be imprinted on its
>   luminous surface.[9]

Ephrem represents one strand in the rich tapestry of the Oriental Orthodox Churches. We might also encounter the Other in writings from the Armenian tradition, especially in the well-loved writers Gregory of Narek and Nerses Shnorhali.[10] For a modern restatement of Coptic spirituality we might discover Matthew the Poor,[11] and for a dazzling insight into Byzantine spirituality turn to the compilation the Philokalia.[12]

Venture north

Seraphim of Sarov (1754–1833), the woodcutter-mystic, invites us to the deep mysterious forests of Russia. A staretz or spiritual elder of the Russian Orthodox Church, his prophetic voice has been heard again in recent years and his sayings are memorable and enlivening. He said, 'Have peace in your heart, and thousands around you will be saved.' He saw clearly the goal of spirituality: 'The aim of Christian life is the acquisition of the Holy Spirit.'[13] Like the eleventh-century Simeon the New Theologian before him,[14] he taught that the heart of Christian prayer was the radical welcoming within the soul of the Holy Spirit, 'the Lord, the Giver of Life'. Witnesses saw Seraphim sometimes bathed in an indescribable light when he prayed for the Spirit. To enquirers who came to him seeking counsel, Seraphim spoke of the vital experiential dimension of prayer involved in the opening of oneself to the divine Spirit. For Seraphim, the heavenly Spirit can be received within: the divide between heaven and earth melts away when the Spirit is present.

Venture south

A safari into the thought-worlds of African spirituality will challenge us on many fronts. It has been said of Africa, 'religion is more danced out than thought out . . . African Churches characteristically celebrate rather than cerebrate the faith.'[15] The rhythmic dances of prayer and the unfettered expression of emotion, of weeping and laughter, challenge stuffy Western approaches where rigid, controlled liturgy is a symptom of our unfreedom. African spirituality is embodied and full-blooded, incarnate, holistic, appreciating physicality in worship. But the spiritual world is not faraway in some distant heaven: there is a keen everyday awareness of the spiritual domain that embraces the realm of the ancestors. Christian spirituality here is marked by a sense of community that transcends time and space. In the African world view, too, angels and demons are close at hand. As it emerges freed from the shackles of colonialism, and empowers women more meaningfully, African spirituality displays an energy and vivacity that questions its staid Western counterpart. A poem entitled 'Roots' by Wandera-Chagenda, the poet from East Africa, echoes some themes raised by the Syrophoenician woman, raising questions of how we view the Other:

> Who are you
> Charcoal-back man?
> They ask.
> I am one
> Whose spirit you have exiled
> Still, and hold in bondage,
> One whose gods you have outlawed!
>
> . . . For centuries my spirit dwelt
> In undisturbed repose.
> The sanctuary
> Of my homestead
> Was protected jealously
> By warrior-ghosts
> Who in the nearby oak tree
> Half-slept out the day.

Until you came
Unprompted
Uninvited
Bent on sheer destruction.

I am not
A mere consumer of your culture,
But I want to build
And to create
And to invent.
I need my roots
I need a firm foundation,
Point of swift departure . . .
In this changing world
I need my own traditions.
These are they
That make me who I am.
Can you tell me who I am?[16]

The tradition of liberation spirituality, flowering amid the oppressed peoples of South America, also overcomes the divide between contemplation and action. These Christians aim to be 'contemplatives in action', forging amid struggle patterns of prayer that are catholic yet provisional:

There is no ready-made path in spirituality, even when we follow masters and schools, ancient and modern . . . there is no ready-made path, but Jesus is the Way . . . there is no need to wait for maps to replace our. spirituality or to stop us from creatively exploring new heights or greater depths . . . our spirituality is an adventure into the unknown, a struggle with all the risks, the greatest throw of our freedom; it is both the meaning of and the quest for our being.[17]

Venture west

One dimension of the shift to which we are called is towards a non-dualistic way of relating to creation. We are being summoned from a pragmatic and self-centred consumer mentality, so deeply entrenched in our culture and mindset, to seeing creation as not an entity to be manipulated or exploited but a divine presence to be honoured. One of the key concepts in the writings of Hildegard of Bingen (1098–1179), poet, mystic and musician, is 'greening' or *viriditas*. Today we talk about the greening of the planet but 900 years ago Hildegard celebrated the presence of the Holy Spirit in the created order through the idea of greening: 'the earthly expression of the celestial sunlight; greenness is the condition in which earthly beings experience a fulfilment which is both physical and divine; greenness is the blithe overcoming of the dualism between earthly and heavenly'.[18] For Hildegard, the wetness or moisture of the planet, revealed in verdant growth, bespeaks the Holy Spirit who 'poured out this green freshness of life into the hearts of men and women so that they may bear good fruit'.[19] She invites us to see the world differently – she even overcomes the dichotomy of heaven and earth by glimpsing the heavenly action in the freshness of the planet, which mirrors the human soul.

In the next century Francis of Assisi displayed a remarkable kinship and sense of unity with creation. At the dawn of capitalism and a creeping consumerist approach to things – Francis was the son of a wealthy cloth merchant and worked in his shop – he discovered a deep connectedness to all things that was honouring and non-exploitative. In his *Canticle of Creation* he hailed the sun as brother and the moon as sister; he greeted Sister Water and Brother Wind and in his ministry he approached the fearsome wolf of Gubbio as 'brother'. Franciscan prayer nurtures such an appreciative and respective approach to the world of nature and overcomes what Martin Buber last century characterized as an 'I–It' relationship, nudging us towards an 'I–Thou' relationship. The former regards the other as an object to be studied or utilized for our benefit; the latter sees the Other as subject in his or her own right who might just change us in the course of genuine encounter.[20] Francis invites us, indeed, to move from a I–Thou relationship that still distinguishes and separates towards a communion with the Other, symbolized in his embrace of the despised leper.[21] He invites us to recognize and celebrate the radical and essential interconnectedness of all things and all people.

Centring prayer is a recent example of a way of praying in the West that encourages a deep realization and experience of the God within. It suggests that by the inward recital of a sacred word – like 'Abba' or 'Shalom' – one can come to a consciousness of the very presence of God within the soul. That is the big shift – we have to overcome our fear that having God so close might hurt. We have to overcome our need to be in control, keeping God at arm's length where he can't actually touch us or disturb us. The word becomes a symbol of one's yearning for God or one's 'intentionality' in seeking to welcome a renewed sense of the indwelling God, and opens oneself up to the divine action within, healing all dichotomy.[22]

Cross the oceans

Ultimately the Syrophoenician woman summons us to risk engaging with other religious cultures entirely. Matthew calls her a Canaanite, a pagan, while Mark locates her in the Phoenician culture in Syria. She represents other religious paths and cries out to us to risk an interfaith encounter with different religions. Jesus shows us how we can move from hesitation to receptivity as he listens to her, hears her and revises his thinking. Note that he doesn't ask the woman to convert, to become a disciple: he moves to unconditional acceptance and a healing of her daughter without preconditions. He is prepared to take her as she is, on her own terms. Step by step Jesus moves to a place where he allows himself to be surprised, delighted even shocked by her. This interfaith encounter invites us to engage with the Other.

We can be heartened in this task by those who in recent years have had the courage to be intrepid spiritual explorers. An outstanding example of one prepared for engagement with Islam is found in the person of Bishop Kenneth Cragg (1913–2012), whose ministerial journey took him across many borders, from Birkenhead to Beirut, from Canterbury to Cairo. His many works provide a powerful resource and stimulus in the privilege of engaging with the Muslim tradition today.[23]

A quite different journey was undertaken by the Catholic Benedictine monk-priest Henri Le Saux (1910–73), who after years of exploring the Hindu tradition took the name Abhishiktananda and lived at an ashram in Tamilnadu, and later as a solitary in the Himalayas. He was concerned to move beyond an intellectual appreciation of Hindu religion into an experiential discovery of Hindu spirituality, especially as witnessed by the non-dualistic advaitic experience of the One Self. His writings do not mask the tensions that arise between the Christian tradition and Hindu perspectives.[24] For Le Saux, interfaith dialogue entails the risk of authentic spiritual encounter that can be both unnerving and exhilarating. He has been called 'an intrepid pioneer on a spiritual frontier'.[25] Bede Griffiths is another example of one who was prepared to receive the insights of the Hindu spiritual tradition.[26]

Thomas Merton (1915–68) exemplifies this courageous and sensitive spirit in relation to engaging with the Asian tradition, particularly with Zen Buddhist spirituality, which he found to have close affinities with the teaching of the desert fathers.[27] A Trappist monk based in Kentucky, his solitude led him to engage with vital issues of social justice and human-rights issues, and in the last decade of his life he was drawn to explore the Zen tradition experientially. Indeed, Zen emphasizes experience and decries intellectual conceptualization, verbalization and rationalization. It is the prayer experience, not doctrine, that fascinated Merton – Zen's sense of consciousness, awareness of the unity of all things, to which Christian contemplation can also lead. In his final journey Merton met the Dalai Lama a number of times, who said of him, 'This was the first time that I had been struck by such a feeling of spirituality in anyone who professed Christianity . . . It was Merton who introduced me to the real meaning of the word "Christian".'[28]

It was indeed a reciprocal encounter. The Syrophoenician woman beckons us to risk such encounters in our quest for a spirituality for our times. As Merton put it:

Life is made of encounters. A true encounter stimulates questions and answers. When you meet an interesting stranger you find yourself alert and curious. Who is this person? You seek to discover something of the mystery of his identity and of his history . . . you begin to open up to him and to share with him the secret of your own life. In this way, a true personal encounter brings us not only knowledge of another, fellowship with another, but also a deeper comprehension of our own inner self.[29]

Questions for reflection

1 Who is the Syrophoenician woman in your context? How will you get to meet her? What challenges do you expect to hear from her? Consider, for example, if you are older, how will you encounter and learn from young people? How will you get to meet non-Christians?

2 What barriers do you have to cross in order to reach the coastlands, in your context? How will you conquer them?

3 In what ways do you reveal a dualistic either/or way of thinking or acting? Name the divides that infect your mind. Why do you think that dualistic thinking is disastrous, not only for relationships between humans but also for our relationship with God and his world?

4 As you reread the accounts of the encounter with the woman, do you think that Jesus changed his mind? What does this say to your current mindsets?

5 It is easier to point to dichotomies 'out there' in society and point a critical finger. What does it feel like to look into your own heart? Does the Syrophoenician woman lurk with your own psyche? Are there aspects of your own personality you find difficult or suspect? What aspects of your own personality do you need to love and embrace? If we don't connect and love those aspects within, then we will carry on projecting them onto other groups, denominations or faiths. What does your prejudice or hesitation about certain other groups tell you about the need to accept, be generous to, all parts of yourself?

Prayer exercise

Follow up the suggestions above and try something that takes you out of your comfort zone. If possible, visit a different Christian tradition or a different faith tradition to experience their worship and way of approaching the divine. Afterwards, review the experience of praying or worshipping differently. What did it feel like? What new insight into yourself, and into God, did you glimpse?

For further reading

K. C. Abraham and B. Myuy-Beya (eds), *Spirituality of the Third World* (Maryknoll, NY: Orbis Books, 1994).

V. Fabella and D. Kwang-son So (eds), *Asian Christian Spirituality: Reclaiming Traditions* (Maryknoll, NY: Orbis Books, 1992).

Bakole Wa Ilunga, *Paths of Liberation: A Third World Spirituality* (Maryknoll, NY: Orbis Books, 1984).

4

Traversing the risky lake

Jesus issues a double summons that echoes across the centuries: 'Put out into the deep' (Luke 5.4); 'Let us go across to the other side' (Mark 4.35). In this chapter we venture across the treacherous waters of the Sea of Galilee. We explore the place of paradox in Christian prayer and face the shadow side. It seems significant that Jesus first calls his disciples by the shoreline. It is truly a *limen*, a threshold to another world. Standing on the strand, the choppy waters of Galilee lapping at his feet and stretching out before him, Jesus says to the fishermen: 'Follow me' (Mark 1.17). It is as if he wants to lead them away from the safety of the bank to uncharted waters. Jesus teaches from the boat, as if he is about to embark somewhere (Matt. 13.2). At one point we read: 'He told his disciples to have a boat ready for him' (Mark 3.9). Jesus has challenging journeys in store for his disciples.

We are invited to encounter two liminal spaces here. First, the awesome, untameable waters of the lake confront us. In the Ancient Near East the sea was feared as the abode of chaos. The waters are brimming with demons and monsters – we even know their names. Here lurk Leviathan and Rahab (Ps. 74.13–14). For the first readers of the Gospels the very mention of the sea evokes the primordial chaos of Genesis 1: 'darkness covered the face of the deep, while a wind from God swept over the face of the waters' (v. 2). The lake also looks forward to the end: the defeat of the beast in the sea, as in Daniel and Revelation. (Indeed, at the end – Revelation 21.1 – 'the sea was no more'). This is all very much part of the first-century thought-world. Such a mindset can be traced across the Ancient Near East – the Babylonian Epic of Gilgamesh conceives the waters as a place of danger and terror, while the Ugarit texts narrate how Baal battles with the sea-god Yam.

Second, there is the liminal space of 'the other side'. Jesus beckons his disciples across the lake. Have you ever noticed how many times in the Gospels Jesus says: 'Let us go over to the other side'? He asks his disciples to leave the security of Capernaum, a conservative, traditional, mainly Jewish town, and to traverse the waters to go to enemy territory, pagan, heathen Gentile terrain, Greco-Roman land, shores where unclean demoniacs and Gadarene pigs lurk uncontrolled.

The dark basalt hills of the Golan Heights, which come down to the Galilee's eastern shore, look bleak and forbidding from a distance, when viewed from the northern side of the lake, but they turn out to be surprisingly fruitful and fertile. Normally it is a place to be avoided – to go there would contaminate the devout Jew. But Jesus calls his disciples to quit their safety zone and risk encounter with the Other, with those who are definitely 'not us'. Even today the Golan Heights are a no-go military zone. But today, as then, it is as if the two opposite sides of the lake, facing each other across the dangerous waters, want to be in dialogue with each other, each posing its questions to the other. It is as if they want to talk – the two sides actually need each other.

Significantly, Mark tells us that Jesus went directly from his encounter with the Syrophoenician woman to the pagan territories of the Decapolis: 'Then he returned from the region of Tyre, and went by way of Sidon towards the Sea of Galilee, in the region of the Decapolis' (Mark 7.31). The Greek text says 'he went into the midst of the district of the Decapolis'. He was empowered and inspired by his meeting with the Other represented in the Syrophoenician woman to go straight to areas on the very frontier of the Roman Empire – the group of ten cities marked by Greek culture, nine of which lay beyond the confines of ancient Israel (located in present day Jordan and Syria). Jesus led his disciples here that they might discover the Hellenistic way of life so different from Jewish values. Indeed, Jews were often affronted and dismayed by aspects of this foreign world – by the nude wrestling, the gymnasia and the theatres. He wanted them to experience culture shock. Matthew tells us that later Jesus again crossed over to the eastern region beyond the Jordan, and he locates significant encounters and teaching there. The enemy, pagan terrain becomes the land of salvation, for it is in these foreign parts, according to Matthew's perspective, that he meets the rich young ruler (Matt. 19.16–22) and makes his inclusive declaration: 'Let the little children come to me, and do not stop them; for it is to such as these that the kingdom of heaven belongs' (Matt. 19.13–15). Indeed, Matthew tells us (4.25), Jesus' fame spreads through all Syria and he welcomes folk from the Decapolis and beyond the Jordan to hear his preaching and experience his healing (Matt. 4.23–25).

Facing the shadows

The 'other side' can be thought of, too, as the 'shadow side' – the east side of the Sea of Galilee is literally in shadow as the sun rises over the mountains of the Golan, and Jesus' journey here invites us to embrace our 'shadows'. As Jung and others developed this idea, they saw that shadows may not necessarily be entirely negative. Sure, they can represent those darker sides of our personality that we do not wish to show to the world, so we suppress them and alienate them from our day-to-day operations and consciousness – things like anger, a critical, judgemental spirit, fear, avarice, greediness, controlling spirit, crude thoughts, uncertain sexual orientation. These may be distasteful traits that we criticize harshly in others as we project them on to other people, forgetting that they are part of our make-up too. But they could be 'golden shadows' – undeveloped potential, under-appreciated talents or dormant gifts that we haven't been able to give space to in our lives because of time restraints or fear of failure. We may admire these things in others but deny them in ourselves, feeling we couldn't possibly have the capacity to achieve them. We have got stuck on the idea that such accomplishments are impossible for ourselves. We get stranded at Capernaum out of fear.

Jesus' journey to the 'dark side' – where he remained for significant periods and explored the territory – teaches us that we may embrace our shadow and make friends with it:

You have heard that it was said, 'You shall love your neighbour and hate your enemy.' But I say to you, Love your enemies and pray for those who persecute you, so that you may be children of your Father in heaven; for he makes his sun rise on the evil and on the good, and sends rain on the righteous and on the unrighteous. For if you love those who love you, what reward do you have? Do not even the tax-collectors do the same? And if you greet only your brothers and sisters, what more are you doing than others? Do not even the Gentiles do the same? (Matt. 5.43–47)

The 'enemy' may be within – that shadow aspect of our personality that we detest in ourselves. Jesus commends a proper self-respect when he commands, 'You shall love your neighbour as yourself' (Mark 12.31). We need to love ourselves and accept ourselves with the same kind of unconditional love that we see in Jesus as he embraces the prostitute, the tax collector, the 'thief' on the cross. We need to show to ourselves the kindness, gentleness, generosity and compassion that we would like to extend to others. Strategies are available that can help us embrace our shadow side.[1]

Turning contradictions to be fought into paradoxes to be lived

The Christian life seems to consist of contradictions. We are told about our capacity to bear the divine Spirit – that we are made in the image and likeness of God – but we are all too aware of our mortality, limitations, fragility and failure. There is the constant tension between ideal and reality. With St Paul we cry out, 'I do not understand my own actions. For I do not do what I want, but I do the very thing I hate . . . Who will rescue me . . . ?' (Rom. 7.15, 24). We are, in Luther's words, *simul justus et peccator* – justified yet sinful. There are other oppositions we wrestle with. We know we must strive to help build Christian community but are summoned at times to solitude. I must come to terms with the child and adult in me, masculine and feminine sides to my

43

unique personality. Theologians argue about the interplay between nature and grace, others about determinism and freedom, nature vs nurture. God is at once immanent and transcendent, close at hand yet seemingly faraway. How can we make sense of these contradictions?

What is striking in the Gospels is how Jesus moves to and fro, across and back across the lake – he repeatedly criss-crosses the stormy waters. He wishes to touch and embrace both Jew and Gentile, both the ritually clean and the unclean; he moves between two domains, between two world views, and is at home in either. Again, it is not a case of either/or but of both/and – Jesus is *The Go-Between God.*[2] In his teaching Jesus transforms contradictions into paradoxes: those who want to save their lives will lose them and those who lose their lives will save them; the first will be last and the last first; God will exalt the humble and meek and cast down the mighty from their thrones; he makes his sun to rise on rich and poor alike, righteous and unrighteous. The parables declare that weed and wheat are to be permitted to grow together; the beatitudes proclaim that the weeping will laugh and the poor possess heaven. The kingdom of God is a topsy-turvy kingdom, both 'now' and 'not yet'. Things are inside out, round the wrong way, at least to conventional thinking – this is a subversive wisdom that undermines usual patterns of thought.

The apostles were described as those who 'have been turning the world upside down' (Acts 17.6). Paul talks about strength made perfect in weakness and foolishness that confounds the world's wisdom. He affirms the paradox, 'For you know the generous act of our Lord Jesus Christ, that though he was rich, yet for your sakes he became poor, so that by his poverty you might become rich' (2 Cor. 8.9). He sees the Christian vocation in highly paradoxical terms:

> We are treated as imposters, and yet are true; as unknown, and yet are well known; as dying, and see – we are alive; as punished, and yet not killed; as sorrowful, yet always rejoicing; as poor, yet making many rich; as having nothing, and yet possessing everything. (2 Cor. 6.8–10)

It is the identity of Jesus that holds the clue. Paul describes Jesus as 'descended from David according to the flesh ... declared to be Son of God with power according to the spirit of holiness by resurrection from the dead' (Rom. 1.3–4). Somehow he is both Son of God and Son of Mary. Crazily, he turns out to be both human and divine, the immaterial Word became flesh. The incarnation smashes into pieces the divides between flesh and spirit. Now all is one in Christ. As in the Orthodox icon of the descent into hell, where the risen Jesus extends one hand to Eve and one to Adam and pulls them out of their tombs to new life, Jesus unites the paradoxes: 'in him all things hold together' (Col. 1.17). At his baptism heaven is torn open – heaven and earth themselves are brought into a new relation. As the *Gloria* puts it, 'Heaven and earth are full of your glory!' Jesus is the lion and the lamb, victim and victor, wounded healer, servant leader, the king who reigns from the cross, alpha and omega. He models a unity of action and contemplation, busyness and stillness. His journey to the other side and his sojourn in the Decapolis where he makes the deaf hear and the dumb speak (Mark 7.37) show us that contradictions can turn to paradoxes, and wholeness comes from uniting opposing elements.

Paradox in spirituality and faith

Paradox lies at the heart of Christian belief. Christmas carols communicate something of the astonishment and wonder at this:

> O wonder of wonders, which none can unfold:
> The Ancient of Days is an hour or two old;
> the Maker of all things is made of the earth,
> man is worshipped by angels, and God comes to birth.[3]

The Nicene Creed declares that 'Light from Light' was 'crucified under Pontius Pilate'. So too the Good Friday hymns of the Orthodox Church delight in the paradoxes of the cross:

Today He who hung the earth upon the waters is
  hung upon the Cross.
He who is King of the angels is arrayed in a crown of
  thorns.
He who in Jordan set Adam free receives blows upon
  His face.
The Bridegroom of the Church is transfixed with
  nails.
The Son of the Virgin is pierced with a spear.
We venerate Thy Passion, O Christ.
Show us also Thy glorious Resurrection.[4]

Celebrate paradox

In the history of Christian spirituality, one of the greatest exponents
of paradox was the mystic Meister Eckhart (1260–1327). Cyprian
Smith tells us:

> Eckhart keeps us perpetually swinging from one pole to
> the other; he will not let us rest in either. To rest in one and
> forget the other is to lose hold of the truth, which is essen-
> tially paradoxical. God is everything, but nothing; distinct
> from creation, yet indistinct from it; there is tension between
> action and contemplation, withdrawal and involvement, silence
> and speech, being and nothingness. Having made a statement
> Eckhart will often go on to deny it; but the truth lies neither
> in the affirmation nor the denial, but in the tug-of-war
> between the two.[5]

It is the key to unlocking knowledge of God:

> This swinging rhythm or oscillation between unlike poles,
> breathing in and breathing out, speaking and remaining
> silent, doing and resting, is the basic rhythm of the spiritual
> life, and it is only within the rhythm that we can know God,
> experience him, think and talk about him. If we abandon
> ourselves to this rhythm, let ourselves be carried by it, it will
> gradually kindle with us the spark of Divine Knowledge.[6]

Eckhart invites us to discover the depths:

> Think of the soul as a vortex or a whirlpool
>> and you will understand how we are to
> Sink
>> eternally
>>> from negation
>>>> to negation
>>>>> into the one.
> And how we are to
> Sink
>> eternally
>>> from letting go
>>>> to letting go
>>>>> into God.[7]

Delighting in the imagery of sea and lake he goes on:

> The highest work of God is compassion.
>> And this means that God sets the soul
> in the highest and purest place which it can occupy:
> in space,
> in the sea,
> in a fathomless ocean,
> and there
> God works compassion.[8]

Convert contradiction

Seventeenth-century England gives us an outstanding example of how paradoxes can be turned into prayer. The Anglican poet–priest George Herbert (1593–1633) wrote that his poems were 'a picture of the many spiritual conflicts that have passed betwixt God and my soul'.[9] His poems testify to an ongoing struggle to accept personally within himself God's unconditional love. He wrestled with a sense of spiritual confusion, the dilemma of unanswered prayer, and found himself echoing the sentiments of Jeremiah and the psalmists.[10]

He discovered prayer to be a place of utter transparency before God, that in prayer there is no place for false pleasantries. In prayer we come before God just as we are; we lower our self-protective barriers, those shields we put up to sheathe ourselves from others. Herbert comes before God with all his woundedness and fragility, and is prepared to speak out in prayer all his questions. Like the once-confident disciples on the lake, Herbert experienced that one of the greatest gifts in prayer is that of utter vulnerability to God. Like Peter he discovered new reserves of courage in the very midst of knowing his weakness. The prayer time becomes a liminal place of transformation – he is undone and remade.

In his poem 'Longing', Herbert lays bare his soul's paradoxes and confesses that to him God seems absent, aloof, faraway, and unresponsive:

> With sick and famish'd eyes,
> With doubling knees and weary bones,
>   To thee my cries
>   To thee my groans,
> To thee my sighs, my tears ascend:
>   No end?
>   [. . .]
>
> Thou tarriest, while I die,
> And fall to nothing: thou dost reign,
>   And rule on high
>   While I remain
> In bitter grief:

But he finds that he can conclude:

> yet am I styled
>   Thy child.

Here we see a pilgrimage from paradox to a new sense that all is well. Just as the stormy lake foreshadows the deep waters of death that Christ must pass through, and his own passage to new life through turbulence and uncertainty, so Herbert sees that his questions and the experience of being pulled in different directions all meet in the cross. Indeed, on the cross God has already enfolded and experienced them; he has *felt* them:

> Ah, my dear Father, ease my smart!
> These contrarieties crush me: these cross actions
> Do wear a rope about, and cut my heart:
> And yet since these thy contradictions
> Are properly a Cross felt by thy Son,
> With but four words, my words, 'Thy will be done'.[11]

Herbert teaches us about *movement* in prayer: a movement from questions, burdens, struggles to a place of surrender, an end to resisting. In 'The Collar' he transits from desperation to affirmation, while in 'Evensong' he moves from failure to a fresh perspective. Famously, in 'Love III' he leaves behind a sense of unworthiness and arrives at a place where he experiences acceptance, giving in to God. Repeatedly he discovers that it is at the point of submission, paradoxically, that we discover God's empowerment.[12]

Cross the lake

This is vividly depicted in the disciples' journey across the lake. Peter and the disciples are summoned to quit the place of familiarity and certainty, what Victor Turner calls 'the world of structure'. Capernaum represented traditional values and conventional thinking, the safe and reassuring routines of daily toil and rest, the affirming rhythms of human family life. However, the risky, dangerous space of the lake might just turn out to be the place of greatest discovery. Here on the lake, and across the lake, the disciples will find out about things they could never have discovered on land. You don't learn to walk on water, on land! In our life of discipleship we may find ourselves in a space where we may long with nostalgia for Capernaum, for the traditional and safe. But we discover, instead, that it is precisely here, on the lake, in the unpredictable and unruly place and on the paradoxical other side, that Christ waits to meet us, to reveal himself to us. We will explore these further in the extended prayer exercises offered below. The place of risk becomes the threshold of the divine.

Questions for reflection

(I recommend that you do the prayer exercise before looking at the questions.)

1 What transitions do you see taking place in Peter on the lake? What echo do these have in your own experience?
2 What paradoxes intrigue or confound you in Christian faith or doctrine?
3 What paradoxes or questions do you notice in your own spirituality or prayer life? What are they telling you – about yourself, and about the nature of God?
4 How do you react to being told: 'You don't have to solve paradox, you have to live it'? How liberating do you find the idea of paradox in our faith?
5 In what way might 'demons' turn out to be 'angels'?

Prayer exercise

Write a poem or prayer that expresses the paradox of Christ or your faith journey. Use the carol or Orthodox hymn for your inspiration.

Or

I invite you to play and to pray with paradox. I invite you to pray with 'dragons' and 'demons'. Practise the Ignatian style of prayer, where we are invited to enter imaginatively into Gospel scenes: to place ourselves there, in the action, with Jesus and the disciples and see what happens – literally, to notice, to watch our feelings and responses and let things come to the surface. It is a powerful way of praying, for it releases elements from our personal depths and gives us a chance to reflect on them too.

Praying with 'dragons'

Revisit the story of the disciples on the lake at night (Matt. 14.22–34). There are eight stages of this prayer exercise as we follow through the Gospel account.

1 Embarking

You and the disciples set sail. Jesus tells them to. 'He made the disciples get into the boat and go on ahead to the other side' (v. 22). Climb into the boat. What do you notice as you look around? It is evening – is it dark already? Are the waters inviting or threatening? Visualize the scene as vividly as you can. What are the other disciples thinking? Listen to their chatter. Are they excited or nervous? What are you feeling as the journey begins? Use your five senses. What can you see? Describe the landscape. What can you smell? Can you taste the breeze? What sounds can you hear? What are you touching?

2 Storm

'When evening came . . . the boat, battered by the waves, was far from the land, for the wind was against them' (v. 24). Can you feel the wind blowing through your hair and clothes? Is the sea inky black yet, or still darkening from sunset pink to marine blue? Do you feel safe as the waters turn choppy, thrashing the side of the boat, and as the wind gets up? How are you feeling right now?

3 Fear

You see a vague outline on the surface of the deep – it looks like a man, but it can't be. 'But when the disciples saw him walking on the lake, they were terrified, saying, "It is a ghost!"' (v. 26). Do you feel a spine-chilling sensation, the hairs of your head as it were standing on end? Can you hear your heart thumping? What does it feel like to be afraid? Is there sweat on the palms of your hand? What fears are crippling you right now? Name your fears. Then, when you are ready, hear his voice: 'Take heart, it is I; do not be afraid!' (v. 27). How does that make you feel?

4 Desire

'Peter answered him, "Lord, if it is you, command me to come to you on the water"' (v. 28). What do you want most, right now? What is your heart's desire, your deepest longing, your greatest need, at this point in your life? As Jesus said to the blind man, so

51

he says to you: 'What do you want me to do for you?' (Mark 10.51). What is your honest response to this question, from the depths of your heart? No one else will hear you – say it!

5 Invitation

You feel strangely and inexplicably impelled to go to Jesus, but you know this is suicidal, to climb out of a boat in a dark storm. Jesus says to you, 'Come.' You love the boat: it is yours, you own it; it is where you are in charge, where you like to be, normally; it is where you give orders to the other fishermen – this is your place of safety. But you find yourself moving to the edge of the boat. You are putting one leg over the side.

6 Solitude

'Peter got out of the boat' (v. 29). As Peter does this entirely off his own bat, so you feel now very alone – it is just you and Jesus. The others fade from view and their views hardly count now. You see the blackness; you feel the howling wind; your foot feels the uncertain, heaving surface. As the waters rise and fall, rise and fall, what is the paradox you are wrestling with? What dragons lurk under the waters? What is the sign of contradiction in your life? What is coming up to the surface in your feelings? Name your questions. Name your emotions right now. As the paradox moves you backwards and forwards, to and fro, expose these to the wind, the gale of the Spirit upon the face of the waters. Feel the Spirit-breath whistling in your ears and the divine waves pounding upon your soul. Feel the energy. Let the place of paradox be a vibrant, creative place. Realize you don't have to solve a paradox – you live it. It may feel a risky place, but you are learning to walk on water – the God of the impossible (Luke 1.37) is upholding you.

For as long as you can, stay with Jesus in the darkness. He is not far away. He is within reach, but you are standing alone before him and the raging elements.

7 Handclasp

As you feel you are sinking, Jesus reaches out his hand to you. He holds you. You will be OK. As he had a question for Peter ('why did you doubt?'; v. 31), what is he asking of you? What question do you hear from Jesus?

8 Response

'Those in the boat worshipped him' (v. 33). Getting back in the boat you feel relief that you are, in a sense at least, 'back home', out of danger. What do you want to say to Jesus? Conclude by giving thanks, then let the boat take you safely back to shore – you will never be the same again. 'When they had crossed over, they came to land at Gennesaret' (v. 34).

What do you want to take away from this, and maybe discuss with a spiritual director or soul friend?

Praying with 'demons'

There is a Zen saying about the need to 'take tea with your demons'. When we name our 'demons' they cease to exert negative power over us – we have established a creative relationship with them. So reread the story in Mark 5.1–20; Matt. 8.28–34 or Luke 8.26–37. Allow it to speak to you symbolically of those patches of darkness in your own life that need healing.

He lived among the tombs (Mark 5.3).
What things in your life are leading to death?

The chains he wrenched apart (v. 4).
What agitates you or disturbs you? What stresses you? What menaces you? What do you feel constraining or restricting in your life, holding you down? What is there in you that is desperate to get out, to find release or expression? It may be something negative, like anger; it could be something wholly positive, like unfulfilled creativity, unexpressed emotions, undeveloped talent. The 'demon' may turn out to be an angel (see the chapter on the desert).

He was always howling (v. 5).
What is your heart's cry right now?

[He was] bruising himself with stones (v. 5).
What causes your integrity or peace of mind hurt or harm? What damages your self-image?

He ran and bowed down before him (v. 6).
Turn your focus to the radiant and mysterious person of Christ.

My name is Legion; for we are many (v. 9).
What are the competing claims in your life? Do they pull you apart, pull you in different directions? Do you feel fragmented?

Send us into the swine (v. 12).
What repressed or suppressed elements in you need to be expressed, released? Breathe them out. Let go of them and pass them into God's hands.

So he gave them permission (v. 13).
Name the element that you want to pass into the hands of Jesus. Release your grip on it; picture it running towards the mysterious deep. It does not have to drown; it can swim in the choppy waters; it can fly!

Sitting at the feet of Jesus (Luke 8.35)
Imagine yourself sitting at the feet of Jesus. Let the light of Jesus envelop the darkness and cast a radiance into your soul. Receive whatever he wants to give you. Take some deep breaths to inhale, as it were, his light deep into your shadows. Embrace the wholeness he wants to bring you. Realize you don't have to be perfect. Accept your limitations but let them be bathed in the light of Christ. Know that you have a treasured, cherished place in the presence of Jesus – like Mary, who chose the better part and also sat at the feet of Jesus (Luke 10.39). Jesus has accepted you – accept yourself. Contrast the verbs in the early verses of Mark 5: binding, wrenching apart, breaking in pieces, crying out, bruising. Now the guy is *sitting* – Jesus has brought him to a place of stillness, resting in the new reality. Practise it. Let go of the bruising, cutting, wrenching. Let go, too, of the self-violence, the blaming, judging, comparing. Learn to *sit*, still, at the feet of Jesus. Linger here as long as you can, clothed and in your right mind.

The man's dividedness, represented by the 'Legion', split him apart. He is given a renewed mind. The divided, torn-apart mind has been clothed with 'the mind of Christ'. Now he is integrated, one, because Jesus has given him a new, unifying focus and mission.

To this divided self Jesus brings a radical reordering – a fresh centre of gravity, a refocused centredness, a new identity and a healing unity. As you wait in the silence, allow Jesus to clarify to you a renewed sense of purpose.

Go home to your friends (Mark 5.19).
Allow Christ to give you, again, an overarching vision of what you are to be. How would you sum up your essential vocation in one word? What is the overarching vision and purpose, uniting and integrating your ministry?

Notice that there is no need to quit the other side. Jesus does not invite the man into the boat; rather, he wants him to be at home on the other side – it is OK to stay on the other side for as long as is needed. What does it feel like to be told this?

Tell them how much the Lord has done for you (Mark 5.19).
Is there someone you can talk with about this? Now get up from sitting at the feet of Jesus – take some strides forward into the new future he has opened up for you in this liminal place.

For further reading

E. de Waal, *Living with Contradiction: An Introduction to Benedictine Spirituality* (Norwich: Canterbury Press, 1997).

C. Elliott, *Praying Through Paradox* (London: Fount, 1987).

R. A. Johnson, *Owning your Shadow: Understanding the Dark Side of the Psyche* (London: HarperCollins, 1993).

P. J. Palmer, *The Promise of Paradox: A Celebration of Contradictions in the Christian Life* (San Francisco, CA: Jossey-Bass, 2008).

H. A. Williams, *Tensions: Necessary Conflicts in Life and Love* (London: Mitchell Beazley, 1976).

5

Penetrating Samaria's border

In order to make a journey from Jerusalem to Galilee, Jesus had the choice of three routes. There was the Via Maris, the magnificent Roman road that followed the coastal plain, the main trade route from Egypt to Mesopotamia. This was an undemanding road, favoured by traders and merchants.

A second route followed the Jordan valley. There one could walk in the great rift valley within sight of the river itself. A third route was tricky and unpopular, for it passed through the Samaritan territory. It was difficult in places because these are the central highlands of the country, with steeply sided hills and meandering ravines. Indeed, a valley south of Shechem is called, to this day, the Valley of the Thieves because historically it was a place of ambush and attack. But of course this third route was undesirable from a Jewish point of view because, as John reminds us, 'Jews have no dealings with the Samaritans' (4.9, AV). In Jewish eyes Samaritans were hated pariahs, half-castes, religiously impure, and to take this route would defile and contaminate the Jewish traveller. They were a despised underclass, a bastard people. Ever since the Assyrian deportation of the population in 722 BC and the subsequent repopulating of the area with people of different bloods, Jews looked upon Samaritans with disdain. Samaria had become a hostile no-go area. However, John tells us: 'he left Judea and started back to Galilee. But he had to go through Samaria' (John 4.3–4). Why did he *have* to take this route? What divine imperative impelled Jesus to choose this most treacherous way? It is vital for Jesus to take this route, it is necessary, for one reason alone: Jesus wanted the disciples to have the experience of travelling through liminal terrain where they would be profoundly changed. He was insistent on this passage to Galilee because he wanted his disciples to enter marginal, despised territory where many of their most cherished ideas about God and humanity would be shattered and reconstructed. For Jesus, there was simply no other way. It turns out to be a transitional route in more than one sense. There will be the outer journey taking place, but an inner journey too – unsettling shifts in perception. In John's perspective, Jesus takes his disciples to Samaria for no less a reason than to expose them to radical paradigm shifts, to lead them to a breakthrough in attitudes. He wants to help them transcend traditional categories of thought and liberate them from the straitjackets and prisons of inherited prejudice and stereotyping. Let's look at three such transitions.

From exclusivity to inclusivity

Jesus leads the disciples from denial to embrace, in relation to the Other. Note how John frames the account in chapter 4. Immediately preceding it he says, 'Now a discussion about purification arose between John's disciples and a Jew' (3.25). The issue of purification was a major preoccupation of the Jewish people at this time, and a special concern of the Pharisees. It was about two things: preserving identity in a pagan environment, and worthiness to approach God. Living under Roman occupation, with imperial values, deities and morals gaining increasing influence since Pompey's invasion in 67 BC, the Jewish people had to attend closely to safeguarding their culture and identity. This had been an age-old concern, of course, but now it was an urgent issue once again: how can Jews live as a separate people, retaining their heritage and sense of distinctness, in the midst of occupation by a foreign power? Pharisees sought to preserve purity of *time* through observance of Sabbath, Passover and festivals, and purity of *place* by having strict zones of demarcation around the Temple, designating limits of access for the different groups of women and gentile believers. They preserved purity of *body* by ritual washings and immersion pools (*mikveh*), by adhering to the rite of circumcision and maintaining scrupulous rules about diet and food preparation. These were of central concern and often the subject of Jesus' critique (Luke 11.37; Mark 7; Matt. 23).[1]

The issue of purity was essentially about boundaries and barriers: who belongs or not; who are to be welcomed as insiders or rejected as outsiders. It was not only a cultural but a religious concern, for only the purified, uncontaminated and orthodox were deemed fit to approach God in worship. So John notes this concern: 'a discussion about purification'. He follows it by Jesus striding into the most unpurified and defiling environment of Samaria, taking his disciples in his wake. In Victor Turner's terms, Jesus enters the liminal word of anti-structure that is likely to subvert the usual norms and codes of behaviour.

Actions speak louder than words. Jesus chooses to sit down – yes, alongside – a person who is triply suspect. First, the person is a woman. As John notes of the disciples: 'They were astonished that he was speaking with a woman, but no one said, "What do you want?" or "Why are you speaking with her?"' (4.27). They were flabbergasted but didn't have the courage to challenge or even question Jesus. Second, she is a Samaritan, despised in Jewish eyes, a source of contamination. Third, she turns out to be a woman with some experience, having had five husbands and a present lover.

Jesus is crossing boundaries, defying conventions, smashing taboos. His promise to the woman of living water (4.10–14) declares: you are worth it; you are acceptable to God; he wants to fill you with his Spirit.[2] You may have a history – you may have a wider experience than most – but God wants you. No wonder the disciples were astonished – confounded. Their minds had to make a somersault!

The living water promised to the woman is not for the purposes of washing, cleansing or purification. There is no suggestion here that she needs baptismal cleansing, though this had formerly been a concern in chapter 3 and at the start of chapter 4. Rather, Jesus is hailing her potential and her worthiness: 'The water that I will give will become in them a spring of water gushing up to eternal life.' When Jesus looks at this woman he does not look in judgement or condemnation. He celebrates her capacity to bear the living water. He sees the possibilities within. Indeed, one who was an outcast and a reject becomes an evangelist and ambassador for the gospel. Jesus is unlocking the latent gifts in her – soon she will leave her still-empty water jar and rush back into the city saying: 'Come and see a man who told me everything I have ever done!' (4.28).

John is telling us that all people, of whatever ethnicity, orientation or gender, are worthy to become recipients of the living water. And to emphasize this point he has the whole village declaring at the end of the story: 'we have heard for ourselves, and we know that this is truly the Saviour of the world!' (4.42). The Greek word for 'world' is of course *cosmos*. Jesus is a cosmic phenomenon. He is opening to all people, of every background, an equal place in God's kingdom.

It is significant to note that the parable of the Good Samaritan (Luke 10.25–37) has a similar message. It is often interpreted as a call to us to be compassionate and a good neighbour but this is not, in fact, its point. The scandalous message of the parable is that the wounded Jewish traveller or pilgrim is prepared to receive healing, support and nurture from a despised Samaritan. We need to learn to receive from those we regard as abhorrent. We need to discover that vulnerability and grace shown by the Jewish traveller who is ready to accept the touch and encouragement of someone who, up to this point, was regarded as an unclean, contaminating half-caste. The conversion is the opening of the heart to the Samaritan – to the Other. But it is precisely the Other who teaches us the way to be a neighbour and reveals, in the process, the heart of God. We also recall how Jesus journeyed in the borderlands between Samaria and Galilee and honours the doubly marginalized man, the Samaritan leper (Luke 17.11–19).

In this shift, this transition, Jesus asks us to examine our own prejudices and short-sightedness. Where do they come from? What sustains prejudice? Does it have something to do with our own lack of a sense of security in God's love? What is your Mount Gerizim – a people or place that is suspect in your eyes? What kind of people do you find yourself avoiding? Who is the Samaritan woman in your situation? Will you ever find her – dare you go to the well?

From particularity to universality

At the centre of the story, John places a conversation about the place of worship. They are standing at Jacob's Well, which is very close to the ancient holy place of Shechem, where Joshua had renewed the covenant (Josh. 24). They are just a few kilometres from the revered sites of Shiloh and Bethel, where the Ark of the Covenant had rested. They are standing near the foot of Mount Gerizim, venerated by Samaritans as the place where God promised blessing; Mount Ebal, opposite, was a place of curse (Deut. 11.29). The woman opens up the age-old controversy: 'Our ancestors worshipped on this mountain, but you say that the place where people must worship is in Jerusalem' (4.20). How is Jesus to respond? At the start of his ministry he had undertaken a dramatic action to show his views about Mount Zion and the Temple. In fact in John's perspective the very first thing Jesus does in the holy city itself is drive out the sellers from its precincts with the enigmatic words, 'Destroy this temple, and in three days I will raise it up' (2.19). Scholars agree that Jesus' action of casting down the tables in the Temple precinct is best understood as a symbolic prophetic action representing the very destruction of the Temple itself.[3] In John 7 it is Jesus, not the Temple ceremony, who is the source of living water.

What does he now say to the Samaritan woman?

Woman, believe me, the hour is coming when you will worship the Father neither on this mountain nor in Jerusalem . . . the hour is coming, and is now here, when the true worshippers will worship the Father in spirit and truth.

(4.21, 23)

It is almost impossible for us to grasp how earth-shattering this statement is for its first hearers and readers. It turns upside down the most cherished beliefs of the Jewish people about the Temple as the main focus of God's presence. It is as if the mighty Temple itself is being dismantled. In Jerusalem Jesus later saw his vocation in terms of demolition and rebuilding.

> As he came out of the temple, one of his disciples said
> to him, 'Look, Teacher, what large stones and what large
> buildings!' Then Jesus said to him, 'Do you see these great
> buildings? Not one stone will be left here upon another; all
> will be thrown down.'   (Mark 13.1–2)

The massive structure of the Temple had only recently been renewed
by Herod the Great, and looked pretty permanent! In the liminal
place of Samaria, Jesus is leading the woman through a process of
deconstruction of her beliefs to new vision. Jesus is leading us from
a narrow, localized understanding of worship and the presence
of divinity to one that bursts every bound: in the words of the
Eucharistic prayer, God is to be praised 'always and everywhere'.[4]
Two things matter: Spirit and truth – Jesus is the embodiment of
truth (John 14.6) and the giver of the Spirit (John 14.26).

This transition asks us: Does the edifice of your belief system
need to crumble? Is your God too small? Have you unconsciously
confined God to certain places or situations? How open are
you to the idea that the Spirit may be speaking to us today, not
only through the Church but in the world – in situations of pain,
through unlikely speakers?

From physicality to sacramentality

While in Samaria, Jesus encounters a fixation with physical things
and leads his hearers into a radically different way of looking
at the world. Twice the woman is stuck on a literal and physical
hearing of Jesus words: 'Sir, you have no bucket, and the well
is deep. Where do you get that living water? . . . Sir, give me this
water, so that I may never be thirsty or have to keep coming
here to draw water' (John 4.11, 15). But Jesus wants to lead her
from the physicality of the water to its sacramentality, and how it
powerfully symbolizes the gift of God. The physical water, and
the well, speak to Jesus of humanity's deep thirst for things of the
Spirit and God's gracious provision.

The disciples too are utterly bewitched by a concern for physical things. They had gone into the town to buy food (4.8). Upon

their return they urge him, 'Rabbi, eat something' (4.31). 'But he said to them, "I have food to eat that you do not know about." So the disciples said to one another, "Surely no one has brought him something to eat?"' (4.32–33).

Jesus sees food as highly symbolic and sacramental. In chapter 6 John will put on the lips of Jesus: 'the bread that I will give for the life of the world is my flesh' (6.51). There he will be misunderstood and accused of advocating cannibalism. Another response will be to ask for a continual supply of free, fresh bread (6.34). His hearers stay on the level of the physical and cannot glimpse sacramentality. In Samaria he explains: 'My food is to do the will of him who sent me' (4.34). He is not talking about a picnic brought to him but of the deep nourishment and sustenance that comes from moving within the Father's will.

Jesus wants to open the disciples to a new vision and a fresh way of seeing reality. He calls them to lift up their eyes: 'look around you, and see how the fields are ripe for harvesting' (4.35). But he is not talking about Samaritan agriculture – the fields around them speak to Jesus of the growth of the kingdom and the spiritual harvest that has become imminent.

This sacramental way of viewing reality is a dominant theme in the fourth Gospel. Jesus sees wine, vines, water, bread, sunlight and candlelight, even shepherding as speaking of himself. The other Gospels combine to give us the clear impression that this was an outlook on the world that was truly characteristic of Jesus himself. The secrets of the kingdom reveal themselves through parables of seed, mountain, field and sea (Matt. 13; Mark 11.23). Jesus says, 'Consider the lilies, how they grow' (Luke 12.27). The Greek word translated 'consider' means 'turn your attention to this; notice what is happening; take note'. It is a summons to a contemplative way of life, a deeply reflective way of seeing the world, and stands in utter contrast with the way the woman and the disciples see things – they can't see past a bucket of water or a plate of food! 'Take a look around you' Jesus says to the disciples – learn to see things differently.

This transition questions our whole approach to priorities in life. Recent surveys revealed that most people in the UK are chiefly interested in such surface concerns as beauty and halting the ageing process; diet and the threat of obesity; celebrities and their Hollywood lifestyles; property – how to acquire and improve it. All these things remain on the level of the crudely physical. Fewer people were concerned about spirituality and the interior life, though there are signs this is changing.[5] How can we train ourselves to look at the world with different eyes?

Perceptions can change in prayer

Perhaps we can begin by seeing prayer itself differently. Sometimes people talk about 'effective prayer', implying that successful prayer obtains satisfactory results or 'answers'. Some even talk of prayers that perhaps can change God's mind or achieve what we want them to achieve – prayer that makes its impact on heaven. Perhaps it is the other way round: heaven makes its impact on us. Prayer is about allowing God to work on us; prayer is coming to a place where God can change us and even communicate with us.

How, indeed, does God 'answer' prayer? One way is through the body of Christ, lives so surrendered to God, so yielded, that God can take us and use us in beautiful and humble ways. We may find ourselves answers to our own prayers. As we pray we receive that divine nudging, that sense that God is asking something of us in the situation. Prayer becomes not so much petition but self-offering. We find ourselves changed by prayer. Our prayer needs to become receptive, reflective and perceptive.

Recent writers have explored the way prayer is not so much about us changing God's mind as about God changing our minds. Jürgen Moltmann speaks of two ways in which we can come to know about things. In modern scientific methods, he maintains, we know things in order to achieve mastery, to gain possession of our subject. But there is a second way:

Meditation is in fact an ancient method of arriving at knowledge which has not been pushed aside by our modern activism . . . meditation is pre-eminently a way of sensory perception, of receiving, of absorbing and participating . . .

The act of perception transforms the perceiver ... Perception confers communion. We know in order to participate, not in order to dominate.[6]

For John Macquarrie, prayer helps to heal the human experience of fragmentedness and individualistic isolation, enabling the pray-er to see the world as a whole: 'prayer enables us to see things in perspective ... Prayer changes our vision of the world ... Prayer interprets the world.'[7] Rowan Williams describes contemplative prayer as involving 'the project of reconditioning perception'.[8] Fraser Watts and Mark Williams, in their study *The Psychology of Religious Knowing*, are cautious about assigning a directly cognitive role to prayer, but they can see that significant shifts in perception take place in the practice of prayer:

Indeed it is doubtful whether the 'acquisition of knowledge' is at all an appropriate way to describe the cognitive changes that take place in prayer. Prayer is probably better described as the reinterpretation of what is in some sense already known than as an exercise in the acquisition of knowledge.[9]

For Watts and Williams, prayer is 'an exercise in the interpretation of experience', and they find attribution theory helpful in understanding this process, in which religious people attribute events to God.[10] Prayer, especially the quiet, reflective type, becomes the place where real discernment is possible, where we see things with fresh eyes. Ann and Barry Ulanov, in *Primary Speech: A Psychology of Prayer*, write of the transformations in perception that can take place in the course of prayer:

This means we are living now in rearranged form. We are the same persons and yet radically different ... The theme that dominates our lives now is the effort to correspond with grace. We want to go with the little signs and fragments of new being given us in prayer.[11]

Thus prayer entails the risk of change in which, little by little, perceptions are revised, self-acceptance grows and contradictions, if not resolved, become better understood. Effective prayer is, then, not about seeking to influence God but about allowing God to do extraordinary things in us. But it requires of us the ability to silence our own admonitions and advice-giving to God, which can be a feature of intercessory prayer – as if we were advising God what he should do next. It requires us to come to a place of vulnerability and receptivity before God.

Routes to Galilee

The pilgrim in the Holy Land today is faced with the same choice as Jesus: there are still three alternative ways of getting from Jerusalem to Galilee. The speedy Route 6 follows the line of the ancient Via Maris – with its fast dual carriageways and service stations at regular intervals it represents the comfortable option. This route races across the land and there is no need or opportunity to engage with what one is passing. A second route, like that of Jesus' time, follows the Jordan valley. It is more bumpy and has twists and turns in places, but is an efficient way of getting from A to B. Both these routes are taken by tourist buses and pilgrims. There *is* a third way, but few take it – certainly a road less travelled. It is the route through Samaria. Marked by roadblocks, checkpoints and potholes, it takes you through areas of desperate poverty where Palestinian Christians and Muslims eke out a living. This is occupied territory and under Israeli military control.[12] Yet this third way exposes the traveller to the bitter issues that divide the Holy Land today. It gives an unparalleled opportunity to support those who are suffering. It is the way trod by Abraham and the patriarchs; the road that took Jesus to Jacob's Well and to his encounter with the Samaritan woman. Which route would you choose? Dare you go to Samaria?

Questions for reflection

1 Who do you spend time with? Who do you avoid? Who is the Samaritan in your context? Of which prejudices do you need to be healed? How inclusive is your church? Read through James 2.1–7. What does that look like in your situation?

2 What is your experience of being changed – or your perceptions being reshaped – in the course of prayer?

3 How can we learn the art of seeing the world sacramentally?

4 Jesus is accused of being a Samaritan: 'Are we not right in saying that you are a Samaritan and have a demon?' (John 8.48). How would you react if a contemporary equivalent was said to your face?

5 Which route to Galilee would you choose? What does this choice of routes look like in your own situation?

Prayer exercise

Reread John 4.7–14 and, as you do, put yourself in the woman's shoes.

First, imagine in your mind's eye the woman leaving her house in the scorching heat of midday – a time she chooses to draw water because she knows no one else will be at the well. See her looking furtively around to see if anyone is scrutinizing her or pointing a finger. Imagine how she feels.

Second, as you picture the Samaritan woman coming to the well at that time, in order to avoid people's judging eyes, reflect on ways you might be tempted to 'put yourself down'. Are there times when you tend towards self-denigration or self-judgement? Do you find that sometimes you apologize for yourself to others?

Third, ask yourself if there are any people or situations in your daily life that annoy you or where you are tempted to make quick or harsh judgements. Who are the groups you avoid like the plague? Where are the no-go areas in your context?

Finally, take an empty bowl and a jug of water. Let the bowl represent either yourself or one of the groups you were just naming. Slowly pour the water into the bowl. Let this speak to you of their capacity – and your own – to receive the living water of the Spirit. Thank God that he welcomes them, and you, with a love that is unconditional. Thank God that he dignifies us by saying: 'The water that I will give will become in them a spring of water gushing up to eternal life' (John 4.14). End by praying that you, and they, may experience the invigorating water of the Spirit ever more deeply.

For further reading

L. B. Brown, *The Human Side of Prayer: The Psychology of Praying* (Birmingham, AL: Religious Education Press, 1994).

G. Burge, *John: The Gospel of Life* (Grand Rapids, MI: Zondervan, 2008).

K. Leech, *Through our Long Exile* (London: Darton, Longman & Todd, 2001).

B. E. Schein, *Following the Way: The Setting of John's Gospel* (Minneapolis, MN: Augsburg, 1980).

6

Climbing the mountain of encounter

In the Bible, Mount Hermon denotes the northern boundary of the Transjordan, the edge of the Amorite territory, and it marks the border to the terrain associated with the tribe of Manasseh. Today the mountain of the Transfiguration is a borderland in a political sense: here the countries of Lebanon, Syria and Israel meet. In this chapter we explore Mount Hermon as a spiritual borderland, as a place of transition where sky meets soil, where glory and passion mingle. Jesus takes his disciples to a sublimely liminal place, the edge of heaven, the brink of eternity. The barrier between heaven and earth is breached as two worlds meet. The barriers of time are dissolved as Moses and Elijah appear with Jesus and the past encounters the present, embracing the future. Mortality and immortality interpenetrate in the radiant person of Christ. The divine reveals itself in the human and the physicality of Christ's body shines with immaterial light. The mount turns out to be a place of breakthrough, a watershed in the Gospel accounts – a pivotal moment pointing to another mountain, Calvary. Hermon is a 'thin place' where the veils that separate are ripped apart. It is an unpredictable place. One minute the disciples are incandescent with divine light and the next they are soaked in a wet fog.

The peaks of Mount Hermon pierce the blue firmament above. They rise to 3,000 m (10,000 feet) above sea level, and with its close proximity to Caesarea Philippi, the previous scene in the Gospel accounts, most scholars agree that this is the most likely locale for the awesome event we call the Transfiguration.[1] It resonates most clearly with Mark's description: 'Six days later, Jesus took with him Peter and James and John, and led them up a high mountain apart' (Mark 9.2). Mount Hermon is part of the Anti-Lebanon range of mountains and dominates the area. It is stunningly snow-capped for much of the year and clouds enshroud its peaks. Meltwaters from the snow form the origins of the River Jordan, which bubbles up out of its feet at Banias. The mountain is steeply sided, and it is a hard climb to make an ascent into its beauty and mystery. The Bible celebrates the cascading dew of Mount Hermon (Ps. 133.3) and suggests it might be a dangerous place, with its 'dens of lions . . . mountains of leopards' (Song of Songs 4.8).

As we read the accounts, it seems that a fourth disciple is missing. Jesus takes John and James, and Peter, but leaves behind Andrew – two sets of brothers, minus one. It is as if Andrew hangs back to create a space for you or me. We can take his place – we can be the fourth person and join in the hike and in the experience. The different Gospels bring various emphases to the story. Matthew (17.1–9) heightens the drama: the disciples fall on their faces in fear and awe, and the transcendent Christ – whose face 'shone like the sun' (v. 2) – reveals great tenderness as he comes to them, touches them and helps them arise. Here there is the contrast between ultimacy and intimacy. Mark (9.2–10) describes how 'his clothes became dazzling white, such as no one on earth could bleach them'. In his account (9.28–36), Luke gives us Jesus as a model of prayer. We are to learn how to pray from the account of the Transfiguration. Luke's Gospel emphasizes the place of prayer in Jesus' ministry and gives us special insight into Jesus' interior life. Luke alone tells us of the prayer associated with the baptism, the choosing of the twelve, and the Transfiguration. Luke gives us a clear impression of the rhythm in Jesus' ministry between activity and prayer. In Luke, Jesus withdraws to the hills and prays through the night after a demanding period in which great crowds gathered for preaching and healing (Luke 6.12). In the third Gospel the context for Jesus' question, 'Who do the crowds say that I am?' (9.18), is Jesus at prayer. Luke alone gives us glimpses into special moments of prayer for Jesus (Luke 10.21). As Dunn puts it, we should note 'the degree to which Jesus provided a model to his disciples as a man of prayer . . . To be a disciple of Jesus was to pray as Jesus prayed.'[2] Luke tells us that not only did Jesus go up the mount to pray, but the prayer-experience itself became the place of *metamorphosis* – the word we translate as 'transfiguration'. Luke says Jesus: 'went up the mountain to pray. And while he was praying, the appearance of his face changed' (Luke 9.28–29). What changes might we expect in the experience of prayer?

The prayer-event of the Transfiguration resonates very clearly with Arnold van Gennep's three stages of liminality, which cast light on the journey of prayer that each of us can make (see Introduction).

Three movements

Ascent

First, there is the separation. The three disciples separate themselves from the rest of the disciples and they create a distance from the demands of ministry and from the pressing crowds. But they do this as a response to an invitation from Christ – indeed, it is he who is doing the separating: 'Six days later Jesus took with him Peter and James and John, and *led them* up a high mountain apart, *by themselves*' (Mark 9.2). Jesus is drawing them away from the hectic world of Caesarea Philippi and into another world. He is taking them to the wind-blown mountaintop to encounter the untameable God. He is leading them into solitude.

This resonates with our own journey of prayer. Prayer begins with a response to Christ's invitation to go higher. It begins with a decision – the decision to accompany Jesus into the upper reaches of prayer. The ascent of the mountain will take stamina, resolution and determination. There will be plenty of distractions and the temptation to take short cuts. What is needed is singleness of heart to go with Jesus, wherever he leads.

Many spiritual writers have explored prayer as an ascent to God, especially male authors.[3] John Climacus (579–649), the abbot of the monastery of St Catherine's, at the foot of Mount Sinai itself, suggested in his work *The Ladder of Divine Ascent* that there were 30 rungs on the staircase to heaven, 30 virtues to be nurtured. St Bonaventure (1217–74), in his work *The Journey of the Mind into God*, writes of the 'mind's ascent to God'. In the English tradition,

Walter Hilton (d.1396) described prayer in terms of ascending a *Ladder of Perfection*. In the sixteenth century, John of the Cross centres his masterpiece, *The Ascent of Mount Carmel*, on the model of going up to God in prayer. A recurring theme is the necessity for detachment – withdrawal from daily demands in order to enter prayer, conceived as a sacred space, as a different world.[4] In the fourth century, Basil the Great had written: 'Now this withdrawal [*anachoresis* – retreat] does not mean that we should leave the world bodily, but rather break loose from the ties of "sympathy" of the soul with the body.'[5] Basil extols the virtues of making a retreat from activity, for a few minutes, hours or days. He says that, for a season, we have to cut our ties, loosen our grip and grasp on activities, let go of our attachments and of our worries. This is so we can become wholly available to God in prayer.

Transformation

In Arnold van Gennep's and Victor Turner's understanding, the initiate enters into a place of transformation. 'And while he was praying, the appearance of his face changed' (Luke 9.29). The Eastern Church, celebrating the event as the Feast of the Metamorphosis, considers that it is the disciples, not Christ, who are changed. Their perception is enlarged, their understanding is transfigured. Lossky explains:

> The Transfiguration was not a phenomenon circumscribed in time and space; Christ underwent no change at that moment, even in his human nature, but a change occurred in the awareness of the apostles, who for a time received the power to see their Master as He was, resplendent in the eternal light of His Godhead. The apostles were taken out of history and given a glimpse of eternal realities . . . Mystical experience implies this change in our nature, its transformation by grace.[6]

The change occurs in the disciples to the extent that they allow themselves to become not spectators but participants in the divinity revealed to them. The Transfiguration event is truly a *limen*, a threshold of the divine as the disciples are caught up into the radiant light of Christ.

Return

Van Gennep's third phase of liminality is reintegration. Jesus and the disciples descend the mountain, to re-engage with the demands of ministry and to begin the walk towards the way of the cross. For Mark, the event of the Transfiguration is a pivotal moment in the course of his Gospel, and leads to the journey to Calvary. It is significant that, upon the descent from the mountaintop of prayer, Jesus encounters immediately a paschal-like situation of pain and suffering, vividly described by Mark, who notes that the demon-infested boy 'was like a corpse, so that most of them said, "He is dead"' (9.26). Jesus lifts him up and, Mark notes, 'he arose' (v. 27, RSV). This is a dramatic depiction of the death and resurrection that awaits Jesus himself, who now says again of the Son of Man 'they will kill him, and three days after being killed, he will rise again' (Mark 9.31). The experience of mystical or receptive prayer may be for us, too, the catapult into dangerous and demanding situations where we will find ourselves fulfilling Jesus' injunction to 'take up their cross and follow me' – words that preface the event of the Transfiguration (Mark 8.34). So we see that the event is bracketed by predictions of passion. The experience of 'supernatural prayer' – to use Teresa's phrase – is no escape from suffering. Rather, as Moses and Elijah found out for themselves, it may mark a transition into the next phase of costly obedience to God. The foaming demoniac, desperate for healing, awaits the disciples at the foot of the mountain. As Joseph Robinson's hymn puts it:

> 'Tis good, Lord, to be here,
> yet we may not remain;
> but since thou bidst us leave the mount,
> come with us to the plain.

Four challenges

Four striking aspects of the transformation encountered on the mountain challenge us about the degree of openness we have in our own experience of prayer.

Awaken the senses

Luke suggests that the prayer experience of the Transfiguration is a place of awakening, heightened consciousness and alert awareness: 'Now Peter and his companions were weighed down with sleep; but when they were fully awake, they saw his glory' (9.32). The disciples are awakened, dazzled, awestruck, and will never be the same again. They are invited to a wakefulness in which their spiritual senses are put on high alert. They are invited to *look* – gaze on the mystery, open their eyes to the light. They are invited to open their ears and *listen* – the Father's voice, from heaven, calls out: 'listen to him!' (Luke 9.35). They are *touched*: the moisture of the wet mist soaks their skin, and Jesus reaches out his hands to them to touch them and lift them up. There is an awakening of the spirit and the body – a coming fully alive, aware and responsive to what God wanted to offer them in this prayer experience. Bonaventure writes that prayer requires the rediscovery of the spiritual senses:

> when the inner senses are restored to see the highest beauty, to hear the highest harmony, to smell the highest fragrance, to taste the highest sweetness, to apprehend the highest delight, the soul is prepared for spiritual ecstasy through devotion, admiration and exultation.[7]

This is the invitation of prayer.[8]

Welcome the displaced

Moses and Elijah enter the prayer of Jesus and he greets them and talks with them. Interpreters often say they represent the Law and the Prophets, but what they have in common is that they are both displaced persons, people in transition. Moses began his life in a basket floating on the Nile – separated from his family home. He later had to quit the Pharaoh's palace and flee to Midian. Leading the exodus journey, he had to spend 40 years wandering in the deserts of Sinai. He did not enter the land of promise but he died on Mount Nebo, tantalizingly close but outside the boundaries of the land.

73

The Letter to the Hebrews celebrates Moses as a pilgrim and wayfarer (11.23–29). Gregory of Nyssa sees Moses as representing the Christian who is continually urged by God to keep moving forward. In his *Life of Moses*, he traces a map of the Christian pilgrimage as it is suggested to him by the Exodus accounts.[9] Ultimately this leads to the ascent of the mountain of divine knowledge, represented in Sinai.

Gregory notices that when Moses climbs a mountain he does not relax in his success but rather finds himself in a position to glimpse the further horizons and greater peaks to which God is beckoning him. From the crest he can view the other mountains he is impelled to climb. So Gregory develops a dynamic view of spiritual development, characterized by *epekstasis* – a vision of the Christian life as continually evolving and progressing, energized by the Holy Spirit. His key text was the resolve of Paul: 'forgetting what lies behind and straining forward [*epekteinomenos*] to what lies ahead, I press on towards the goal, for the prize of the heavenly call of God in Christ Jesus' (Phil. 3.13–14). For Gregory, the disciple should never stand still but continually stretch himself or herself towards the 'upward call' and so reach one's full potential in Christ.[10] Each stage reached in the spiritual journey is but a beginning, not an end – the pilgrim can never say he or she has arrived. In Gregory's eyes, the greatest sin is that of complacency, of resting on one's laurels. Gregory's vision is one of lifelong learning or, rather, eternal progress.

If Moses is present as a pilgrim figure, Elijah too is a displaced person, a person in transit. As the Carmelite Paul Chandler puts it: 'We consider him as a man on a journey, always on the move from "here" to "there" in response to God's call . . . God's grace does not allow him to be still. It calls him to grow and become.'[11]

Elijah's journey had taken him from the Jordan to Zarephath in the far north, from Samaria to Mount Carmel and ultimately, after a long sojourn in the desert, to Mount Horeb, where he hears the still small voice of God at the mouth of the cave: as we saw in Chapter 2, God is not in the fire or whirlwind of Elijah's life but in quietude (1 Kings 19.9–13). And it is precisely in the experience of stillness and solitude that Elijah receives a triple redirection of his life (vv. 15–17) and clues for the next stage of his life's journey. Both Moses and Elijah, then, find themselves in transit, and both discover in the midst of the transit the life-changing experience of theophany – the encounter with God – on the mountains of Sinai and Horeb.

In his mountaintop experience, Jesus welcomes the pilgrims Moses and Elijah into his prayer-space and talks with them about the exodus he is to accomplish in Jerusalem (Luke 9.30–31). The time of prayer becomes for Jesus a dialogue with God through these pilgrim figures, and so the mount of the Transfiguration points to the mount of Calvary. This suggests that prayer can be for us, too, where we learn to hear the voices of the displaced and allow them to disturb us with references to the cross in our lives.

Still body and mind

Peter's instinct is to construct tents – to domesticate the divine, to contain the mystery, to regain control in the situation: 'Let us make three tents' (Luke 9.33, ESV). This can represent our attempts in prayer to 'get a handle' on God, to box God in with words, concepts and images, to encase divinity with human structures. But precisely at the point when Peter suggests this, 'a cloud came and overshadowed them; and they were terrified as they entered the cloud' (Luke 9.34). The response to human tent-building is a divine smothering or drenching in mysterious wet mist where visibility is reduced to nil. The cloud now dampens the senses and exuberant conceptualizing and silences the overactive mind. It eclipses the sun – there has been, as it were, a change in the weather, from bright sunlight to darkening cloud, gloom and impenetrable haze. A swirling fog blankets the disciples. This expresses well the sense of disorientation and confusion one experiences in a baffling liminal place. In the cloud one feels out of control, not knowing which way to turn. It turns out to be a poignant symbol of that transition in prayer from active, discursive thinking to simpler loving. Peter's unfulfilled desire to construct three tents resonates with Turner's idea that the liminal space is an 'antistructure', where normal responses or default-type reactions will not do: Peter certainly discovers the cloud to be a place of unlearning and undoing as his normal controlling instincts are quenched.

Enter the cloud

The overshadowing cloud that envelops Peter and the disciples evokes the awesome cloud that enshrouded Moses on Sinai (Exodus 19.16). Gregory of Nyssa says: 'Whoever looks to Moses and the cloud, both of whom are guides to those who progress in virtue . . . advances to the contemplation of the transcendent nature.'[12] He goes on:

> For leaving behind everything that is observed, not only what sense comprehends but also what the intelligence thinks it sees, it keeps on penetrating deeper until by the intelligence's yearning for understanding it gains access to the invisible and the incomprehensible, and there it sees God. This is the true knowledge of what is sought; this is the seeing that consists in not seeing, because that which is sought transcends all knowledge, being separated on all sides by incomprehensibility as by a kind of darkness.[13]

The classic fourteenth-century text *The Cloud of Unknowing* invites us to experience the cloud of prayer. The author pursues a similar apophatic approach: the *via negativa*, cautious about the use of vivid images in relation to speaking of God – indeed, commending wordless silence rather than exuberant speech.

> When you first begin, you find only darkness and as it were a cloud of unknowing. You don't know what this means except that in your will you feel a simple steadfast intention reaching out towards God . . . Reconcile yourself to wait in this darkness as long as is necessary, but still go on longing after him whom you love. For if you are to feel him or to see him in this life, it must always be in this cloud, in this darkness.[14]

The *Cloud* equips the reader with a vocabulary with which to articulate the inner stirrings of prayer. It offers a framework of beliefs as a tool with which to begin naming and making sense of subjective experience. The *Cloud* works with a psychology of the time, with its theory about the faculties of the soul (chapters 62–66). It highlights the importance of the will in responding to God and downplays the role of imagination and what it calls 'sensuality'. It pays attention to the affective aspects of prayer rather than the cognitive aspects, and says of God: 'He may well be loved, but not thought. By love he can be caught and held, but by thinking never.'[15]

The *Cloud* aids the identification of 'signs' of spiritual progress or impediments to growth. It teaches that there are various signs, clues or evidences that suggest that the reader may be ready to make a transition in his or her praying from discursive, active thinking with words and images, as in meditations on the passion, towards the wordless silence and solitude of contemplation. One key indicator is that of desire or yearning:

> It seems to me, in my rough and ready way, that there are four states or kinds of Christian life, and they are these: Common, Special, Solitary, and Perfect . . . I think that our Lord in his great mercy has called you in the same order and in the same way, leading you on to himself by your heart-felt desire.[16]

The *Cloud* offers guidelines for the task of discernment, to be worked through with a 'discreet director'. Sometimes it will be necessary to exercise extreme caution in interpreting unbidden feelings: 'All other comforts, sounds, gladness, sweetness that come suddenly to you from outside . . . please do suspect! They can be good or evil; the work of a good angel if good, and of an evil angel if evil.'[17] The author wants to urge the Christian to step forward into a transfiguration kind of prayer characterized by watching, waiting, longing: 'So when you feel by the grace of God that he is calling you to this work, and you intend to respond, lift up your heart to God with humble love . . . It all depends on your desire.'[18]

There are other clues or indicators that suggest that someone may be ready to enter more mystical, receptive prayer, which resonate with what we saw Teresa teaching earlier in the move into the room of supernatural prayer. One finds oneself unfulfilled by Peter's tents, representing prayer hemmed in by words. Even liturgical prayer or the daily office or traditional devotions come to feel constricting and stifling. The 'cloud' beckons.

Questions for reflection

1 Are you most comfortable with a model of prayer as ascent to God or an approach that celebrates God's immanence?[19]
2 What are the helpful aspects of seeing prayer as ascent? What aspects are less helpful?
3 As you reflect on your own personal faith history, where have you discovered moments of transfiguration or transformation? Could you describe them as a liminal period?
4 What is your experience of 'praying in the cloud' or the apophatic mode of wordless prayer? Are you tempted, like Peter, to build 'tents' in your prayer times? What do they symbolize for you?
5 If the Christian journey is about 'straining forward to what lies ahead' (Phil. 3.13–14), what do you glimpse as the next mountain to climb?

Prayer exercise

This exercise is in two parts. First, use your physical senses to awaken your spiritual senses. Take a prayer walk in creation. Look carefully at what you pass, and watch out for signs of the divine, noticing what speaks to you of God. Look up and look down. Listen to the sounds with what Benedict called 'the ears of your heart'. Taste any fruit or dew, and 'taste and see that the LORD is good' (Ps. 34.8). Enjoy the fragrances. Touch different surfaces and look for what Bonaventure called 'the fingerprints of God'. Let this be a sensual and sacramental experience, and way to stimulate the practice of your spiritual faculties.

Second, go to a quiet place and shut down your senses, closing your eyes. Feel the darkness and silence your active thinking. Breathe slowly and become aware of your breathing. Try to quieten your mind and listen. Become receptive to divine whispers. Rest in this 'cloud' for as long as you can.

Afterwards, make a review of your prayer time. What did you find easy and what difficult? Where did you most sense God?

For further reading

A. Andreopoulos, *This is My Beloved Son: The Transfiguration of Christ* (Brewster, MA: Paraclete Press, 2012).

T. M. Gallagher, *An Ignatian Introduction to Prayer: Scriptural Reflections According to the Spiritual Exercises* (New York: Crossroad, 2008).

R. Haughton, *Passionate God* (London: Darton, Longman & Todd, 1982).

M. B. Pennington, *Lectio Divina: Renewing the Ancient Practice of Praying the Scriptures* (New York: Crossroad, 1998).

7

Discovering the forgotten threshold

For many, many years it has puzzled biblical interpreters and preachers: why did Jesus send the blind man of John chapter 9 to the Pool of Siloam? This has been a conundrum on several levels. First, Jesus does not heal the blind in this way in other accounts. To be sure, there are several stories about the cure of closed eyes – we think, for example, of blind Bartimaeus (Mark 10.46–52). Jesus even uses spittle on one other occasion (Mark 8.22–26). But here, after anointing his eyes with clay from the earth, he commands the blind man to go down to the Pool of Siloam and wash. What would be the significance of that? Second, archaeologists have long been confused over the function of the narrow pool they saw named Siloam. Was it something to do with the city's water supply, given its proximity to the ancient water source for Jerusalem, the Gihon spring? Hezekiah had brought this water supply within the city during the Assyrian threat and it is still possible to walk through the 68 m (225 feet) of the tunnel that now supplies Siloam. Was its purpose, then, to provide access to this supply so it could be used for domestic purposes?

In 1992 the respected archaeologist Jerome Murphy-O'Connor wrote: 'The original form of the pool has been lost forever.'[1] But since 2004 stunning archaeological discoveries have been made at the pool that reveal its true extent and its real function: it is a *limen*, a threshold, for pilgrims entering Jerusalem after their dirty and exhausting trek through the desert. We shall take a fresh look at this story and, for the first time, explore its astonishing role in the spirituality of the episode.

The site in question is the lowest point of the ancient city of David, which first developed on the southern spur of the Ophel ridge around 1000 BC. While the Temple came to be built at the top of the ridge (the high place), this site developed at the foot of the hill, on its southern edge. Visitors to what has been called in the past the Pool of Siloam have been shown a narrow, oblong-shaped pond of Byzantine age. In the fifth century, Empress Eudokia built a basilica over this pool to celebrate the miracle of John 9. The basilica has long disappeared – destroyed by the Persians in 614 – and all that can be seen is an unimpressive pool measuring just 3 m (10 feet) across, with a few stumps of the basilica's pillars remaining.

In the summer of 2004 the Israeli archaeologist Eli Shukron began to take another look at the ground just south of this site because work needed to be done to improve Jerusalem's drainage system. Some huge stone ledges cut into the rock were discovered. Archaeologists continued to dig and identified several flights of steps leading to a vast open pool. These had been covered over with mud and debris sliding down the hill since the end of the first century. This site was probably abandoned after 70 AD, when Titus destroyed the Temple.[2]

As excavations continued, the scope of the discovery became clearer: this was the real Pool of Siloam – the narrow Byzantine pond, long venerated by pilgrims, was just a feeder bath for it. Each side measures a staggering 68 m (225 feet) – the pool is bigger than an Olympic swimming pool, accommodating a substantial and impressive body of water. Indeed, there was nothing to compare with it within the city of Jerusalem – it was a breathtaking oasis. Three flights of five broad, monumental steps, each flight separated by a wide landing, lead down into the pool. In fact only half of the pool has been excavated,[3] but enough to reveal that the Pool of Siloam was a spacious and inspiring tract of water on the very edge of the ancient city of David. So what was its function?

More than just a reservoir, it was a *mikveh* – a ritual bath or immersion pool for pilgrims arriving in the holy city. It is right next to the gate in the city walls of Jesus' time and marks the entry point for travellers arriving via the Hinnom valley from the west, via the Kidron valley from the east and from the Judean desert. It is literally the threshold of the city, and pilgrims would cleanse themselves here before ascending a steep staircase up to the Temple Mount. This staircase has also recently been revealed by archaeologists and since 2012 it has become possible to retrace the steps of arriving pilgrims and ascend the slope of the original Mount Zion towards the area of the Second Temple. The Pool of Siloam, then, functions only in relation to the Temple itself: it is the ablution pool for sweaty and dirty pilgrims. At the foot of Mount Zion, it is a welcoming place for worshippers.

What are the implications of this discovery for our reading of John 9? What is the meaning of Jesus' words to the man, 'Go and wash in the Pool of Siloam' (v. 7)? And in any case: so what? What does it mean to us today? It turns out to be a triple imperative from the lips of Jesus.

Open your eyes to your true identity, dignity and worth

The first transition or movement for the blind man is both physical and spiritual and touches on his very identity. Jesus wants the man to position himself at the point of the threshold. He will only receive his healing at this place – not even at the place where Jesus first met him. He has to make an act of faith and obedience and get himself down to the *limen*. As he is still deprived of his sight at this stage, he is escorted down the steep hill from the Temple area to this lowest point of the city walls. And he needs to descend those three flights of steps; he needs to wade in the water; to apply the water to his muddy, stinging eyes. What will be the first thing this man sees in his entire life – given he has been blind from birth? His opening eyes will first see a flight of stone steps beckoning him up the hill to the very Temple of God. He will see an inviting staircase leading, it seems, to heaven. And he will know this: he is accepted; he is wanted; a child of God. All his life he has been exiled from the Temple precincts because of his disability – the sick and imperfect were not allowed anywhere close to the Holy of Holies. All his life he has been excluded from the holiest place by man-made regulations but now he sees God's invitation – he sees, as it were, God's hand beckoning him up those steps. This was Jesus' longing: that God's house should be a place for all people. When he cleansed the Temple, driving out the sellers and money-changers in Matthew's account, something astonishing happened to the untouchables: 'The blind and the lame came to him in the temple, and he cured them' (Matt. 21.14).

What a healing needed to take place in those waters of Siloam! Not only the restoration of the man's eyes but the deep healing of his spirit. All his life he had been an outcast, rejected, not good enough – even a threat to the purity of others. He had been stigmatized and ostracized – people would gossip and speculate about him, just like the disciples when they asked: 'Rabbi, who sinned, this man or his parents, that he was born blind?' (John 9.2). To compound his suffering, the man had to live with the guilt of what he may have done to deserve his affliction. Jesus was emphatic: 'Neither this man nor his parents sinned; he was born blind so that God's works might be revealed in him' (v. 3). In John's perspective this episode is not a miracle but a sign – an indicator of the type of kingdom Jesus came to inaugurate.

Today we experience rejection on many counts. We may be rejected because of the colour of our skin, our sexual orientation or because we don't fit in with other people's expectations. We might be bullied, teased or ridiculed or just ignored and sidelined. The important thing, which the man discovered at Siloam, is that our self-worth does not come from what other people say about us. It comes from what God says about us, and he declares that in Christ we are beloved, cherished and wanted; we are unique and irreplaceable. As John affirms, 'See what love the Father has given us, that we should be called children of God; and that is what we are' (1 John 3.1).

Discover yourself to be a pilgrim

The second imperative of Jesus to the man sent to the Pool of Siloam requires the man to stand where pilgrims stand, at the very threshold of the approach to the holiest place. He is to locate himself precisely at the place where pilgrims arrive from their dusty and exhausting journeys; he is to discover for himself the joy and exhilaration of becoming a pilgrim to the holy place. This is a transition from being a nobody, a nonentity, to becoming a worshipper desired by God – now he takes his rightful place among the pilgrim people of God, finds himself walking in the footsteps of Abraham and David, on a spiritual quest and a spiritual journey.

He ascends the flight of steps towards the crest of the holy hill, towards the Temple sanctuary, its white walls glistening in the sunlight. He had been barred from here all his life and now his heart is thumping with excitement and joy. Like the man at the Pool of Bethesda (John 5) who had been rooted to that spot for 38 years, the man born blind had had little experience of movement at all, confined to one specific locale on the outskirts of the Temple area where he simply sat and begged (John 9.8). But now, ascending the staircase to Zion, he discovers himself to be a person in motion, in movement. He discovers himself to be a pilgrim and can for the first time celebrate the psalm of ascent: 'I was glad when they said to me "Let us go to the house of the LORD!" Our feet are standing within your gates, O Jerusalem!' (Ps. 122.1–2). He is empowered by Christ. Where formerly he had been a passive recipient of alms, now he can take responsibility for himself as he steps confidently towards the Temple sanctuary.

For Christians, the Pool of Siloam evokes the liminal waters of baptism, an important theme in John's Gospel. The truths declared by baptism resonate strongly with the story of John 9. Baptism proclaims that all are welcome in God's new family, invites us into waters of inclusion and acceptance. In baptism, Paul stresses, all human distinctions are put aside:

> As many of you as were baptized into Christ have clothed yourselves with Christ. There is no longer Jew or Greek, there is no longer slave or free, there is no longer male and female; for all of you are one in Christ Jesus.   (Gal. 3.27–28)

The baptismal liturgy affirms that we are made children of God. It declares that we are joining a new community; gives us a new identity in Christ; forms us into pilgrims. As the baptismal prayer puts it:

> May God, who has received you by baptism into his Church, pour upon you the riches of his grace, that within the company of Christ's pilgrim people you may daily be renewed by his anointing Spirit, and come to the inheritance of the saints in glory. Amen.[4]

The waters of baptism are truly a liminal place, for in them we leave behind an old way of life without Christ and through them we encounter the transforming Spirit. As we emerge, dripping, from the font or baptismal pool, we are setting out on a journey. As the rite puts it:

> . . . today God has touched you with his love
> and given you a place among his people.
> God promises to be with you
> in joy and in sorrow,
> to be your guide in life,
> and to bring you safely to heaven.
> In baptism God invites you on a life-long journey.
> Together with all God's people
> you must explore the way of Jesus.[5]

The baptismal liturgy is clear: 'In baptism these candidates begin their journey in faith.'[6] Baptism has been called 'illumination' or 'enlightenment' by the Eastern Church. It involves opening our eyes to a new reality, enables us to see ourselves differently, changes the way we see the world. Like the man born blind wading through the waters of Siloam, we too are invited to plunge ourselves into the waters of God's life-changing grace.

Wade in the waters of the Spirit

For Jesus, the waters of the Pool of Siloam speak powerfully of the Holy Spirit, for it is in the context of the great Jewish ceremony of *Sichat Beit Hashoeva*, meaning 'the Rejoicing of the water-drawing', the Great Day of the Feast of Tabernacles, that he makes a glorious promise concerning the Spirit of God:

> On the last day of the festival, the great day, while Jesus was standing there, he cried out, 'Let anyone who is thirsty come to me, and let the one who believes in me drink. As the scripture has said, "Out of the believer's heart shall flow rivers of living water."' Now he said this about the Spirit, which believers in him were to receive; for as yet there was no Spirit, because Jesus was not yet glorified.
>
> (John 7.37–39)

Jesus was attending the Temple liturgy where Ezekiel's vision (ch. 47) was proclaimed to the pilgrims – a spring of God's generous blessing bursts forth from under the altar of the Temple and it spills out to bring renewal to the whole world. The water gets deeper and deeper as Ezekiel follows the line of the river from the holy city and out into the deserts. At first the prophet can wade in the water but soon it comes right up to his waist, so he must swim in the river of God's blessing. The Tabernacles festival reached a climax when, on the last day, a solemn ceremony celebrating this vision, carried up to the Temple in a golden vessel waters from the Pool of Siloam. It was a joyous, colourful and noisy procession accompanied by musicians with harp, drum, cymbal and the *shofar* trumpets. The water was poured out as a sign of God's blessing in 'the Age to Come'. Since they originate with the Gihon spring, and one of the rivers of paradise is called the Gihon (Gen. 2.13), the waters came to symbolize the hope of a paradise restored – the waters of Eden will one day flow again. Jesus was watching this ritual when he cried out his urgent, awesome promise. You do not have to wait until the last day. With his glorification on the cross, the Spirit will be unleashed as an overflowing stream to renew all of creation.[7]

When Jesus echoes Ezekiel's prophecy and makes his glorious promise, what does he mean? How can the Spirit come to us as a stream of living water and flow in us and out through us? Jesus alludes to the energy of the Spirit. He is talking of the cascade of the Spirit, the movement of the Spirit, the empowering of the Spirit, his energy within us. He speaks of an inflow and an overflow. The Spirit comes to us and then, bubbling up like a mountain brook, streams out to others. Jesus is talking about the renewing and refreshing grace of the Spirit. As sparkling, living water invigorates and enlivens weary bodies, so the Spirit makes us new, replenishing and restoring parched souls: this is the healing grace of the Spirit, echoing Ezekiel's vision of trees, with leaves for healing, thriving alongside the riverbank (47.12).

Jesus, in his astonishing promise of the river of God, suggests three steps the disciples need to take: 'Let anyone who is thirsty come to me, and let the one who believes in me drink. As the scripture has said, "Out of the believer's heart shall flow rivers of living water"' (John 7.37–38). They must first acknowledge and recognize their thirst for the Spirit. Second, they need to come to Jesus the giver of the Spirit and place themselves in expectant relation to him. Third, they are invited to drink and receive afresh the living water. In our prayer we can take these three steps. In prayer, we can thirst, come to Jesus and drink, receiving afresh the Spirit of God.

According to John's chronology, Christ's promise related to the waters of Siloam was a recent event, taking place not long before he met the man born blind, so his command to 'Go, wash in the pool of Siloam' (9.7) clearly evokes the gift of the Spirit, bubbling up as Siloam's waters themselves emerge from deep within the earth near Gihon's mighty spring. In saying 'Go, wash in the pool of Siloam', Jesus is saying: 'Go, and feel the fresh waters on your skin. Go and drink deep of the Spirit! Open your eyes and see the river of God!' Indeed, part of the water-drawing ceremony at Siloam included the words: 'We belong to God and our eyes are turned to God!'[8] In this third transition, the man born blind moves from spiritual aridity and thirst to the joy of imbibing the divine Spirit.

Ultimately this episode is about seeing. The man, blind from birth, can see again. But what, precisely, can he see? He sees the staircase to the Temple beckoning him to worship as a valued member of the people of God. He sees the gate where tired pilgrims enter the city, sees the steps that lead down to the cleansing waters. And he sees the water, fresh and cool, a mighty sign of the Spirit. Perhaps he takes a swim! I see him splashing and laughing in the water. He is accepting himself as the one he truly is, God's child. And he cries out to himself, 'I belong!'

Questions for reflection

1 What is your experience of rejection? Have you suffered judge-mental attitudes towards yourself, or a labelling like that imposed on the man born blind? Have you ever been made to feel un-worthy in the sight of God? How can we enter the waters and discover Christ's healing today? Do we hold on to any negative self-image that needs to be washed away, like the mud in the man's eyes?

2 The man born blind was invited to rediscover his identity as a pilgrim, cherished by God. How can we live as pilgrims, even if we are not taking a physical pilgrimage?

3 Celebrate the work of the Holy Spirit in your life. Jesus loved the imagery of water. What images or metaphors can you use to describe the inner workings of the Spirit?

4 'Go, wash in the pool of Siloam.' Is there something you must do, some step you must now take, to enter into your healing?

5 The man in our story emerged from the waters to face a beckoning staircase leading to the Temple. To where is God beckoning you?

Prayer exercise

Pour water slowly into a glass bowl as a visual reminder to you of the font or place of your baptism. Reflect on how in the sacra-mental waters God welcomes us and reorientates us. When you are ready, and if you want to, reaffirm your baptismal commitment to God:

To follow Christ means dying to sin and rising to new life
with him.

Therefore I ask:

Do you reject the devil and all rebellion against God?

I reject them.

Do you renounce the deceit and corruption of evil?

I renounce them.

Do you repent of the sins that separate us from God and
neighbour?

I repent of them.

Do you turn to Christ as Saviour?

I turn to Christ.

Do you submit to Christ as Lord?

I submit to Christ.

Do you come to Christ, the way, the truth and the life?

I come to Christ.[9]

Stand for a few moments quietly looking at the surface of the
water. Recall the story of the man born blind wading through the
waters. Give thanks that God wants you as you are and calls you
too to become a pilgrim. Then end with the prayer:

May almighty God deliver us from the powers of darkness,
restore in us the image of his glory, and lead us in the light
and obedience of Christ.

Or

Take the place of the man in the story and retrace his steps
in your imagination. Picture yourself standing at the water's
edge. Pause, and become aware of your need. Bring to mind any
experiences of rejection. Then descend the steps into the water.
Nothing can stop you now – plunge yourself beneath its surface.
As you feel the waters enfold you and surround you, rejoice in
God's enveloping and healing love. Give thanks that he heals our
hurts and affirms us as his children. As you emerge from the pool,
ask yourself where you are to go next. How can you live this out
and share this experience? End with a resolve, like the man in the
story, to share the good news.

For further reading

L. E. Mick, *Living Baptism Daily* (Minneapolis, MN: Liturgical Press, 2004).

S. Platten, *Pilgrims* (London: Fount, 1996).

T. Radcliffe, *Taking the Plunge: Living Baptism and Confirmation* (London: Bloomsbury Publishing, 2012).

R. Reich, *Excavating the City of David: Where Jerusalem's History Began* (Jerusalem: Israel Exploration Society, 2011).

8

Ascending towards the holy city

In the days before his passion Jesus leads his disciples to an extra-ordinary liminal place, the Mount of Olives. It is the bridge between the desert and the city, the link between time and eternity and the intersection between heaven and earth.

First, it is the threshold between the city and the desert, for it marks the ending of the desert and the brink of the city, rising to a height of some 762 m (2,500 feet) above sea level. Bethany, the village of Martha, Mary and Lazarus, lies on the eastern flank of the mountain, facing the desert. The western slope of the mountain, just over the crest from Bethany, faces the holy city itself. The Mount of Olives has been called the numinous threshold of the city, for all pilgrims, as they make their journey up from the deep rift valley to the city, must pause there, to catch their breath and see the amazing panorama of the glistening city below. It is literally and symbolically a watershed: not only does the climate change on this mountain range (desert to the east; Mediterranean type to the west) but also one's very heart and mind change in climbing the mountain in preparation for the encounter with the holy city.

Second, it is the threshold between time and eternity. It is the eschatological mountain, becoming the focus of hope for God's advent at the end of time. Zechariah predicts: 'On that day his feet shall stand on the Mount of Olives, which lies before Jerusalem on the east; and the Mount of Olives shall be split in two from east to west by a very wide valley' (14.4). This is the cataclysmic vision of Zechariah in the sixth century before Christ. In a gentler image he had written, 'Rejoice greatly, O daughter Zion! Shout aloud, O daughter Jerusalem! Lo, your king comes to you; triumphant and victorious is he, humble and riding on a donkey, on a colt, the foal of a donkey' (9.9). In his apocalyptic dream Joel sees God gathering the nations for judgement in the valley below (Joel 3). So the Mount of Olives becomes a place of judgement and hope, but all these dreams look to the far future for their fulfilment. These are visions of the end of times. To this day the Mount of Olives is covered with hundreds of tombs – a vast Jewish cemetery clings to its eastern side, while Christian graves are in the valley and Muslim tombs are by the city walls. All three traditions await the coming of God and the dawn of judgement day at this location. Humanity's longings for a new world are focused here.[1]

Third, related to these hopes, the Mount of Olives, rising steeply towards the skies, is the threshold between heaven and earth. It is from this mountain, according to Luke, that Jesus will make his ascension to the Father in the mysterious cloud (Luke 24; Acts 1).

This is a mountain that pilgrims must cross in order to reach the holy city – there is no other way, from the east. In Hebrew the word for pilgrimage is *aliyah*, meaning 'to go up'. With pilgrims of old we climb towards Jerusalem; with them we make our own the Psalms of Ascent (120–134): 'I lift up my eyes to the hills – from where will my help come?' (Ps. 121.1). 'As the mountains surround Jerusalem, so the LORD surrounds his people' (Ps. 125.2).

The astonishing story of John 11 can only be understood by an appreciation of the theological symbolism of the Mount of Olives.[2] According to John's chronology and geographical perspective, before his final journey to Jerusalem, Jesus positions himself deep in the desert, at the very point of the exodus and of his baptism. John says: 'He went away again across the Jordan to the place where John had been baptizing earlier, and he remained there' (John 10.40). Jesus waits at the very point of the ancient salvation, for it is here at the great river, as we recalled, that Joshua had led the Hebrews into the Promised Land, at the end of their wearisome journey of 40 years (Josh. 3). Jesus is going back to where it all began, as if to suggest that he might be leading a new exodus journey into freedom. It is also precisely the place where he had received that amazing affirmation at his baptism: 'You are

my Son, the Beloved' (Mark 1.11; Luke 3.22). It is the place where
he had seen the heavens torn apart, opening up in his ministry a
new way to God. Now Jesus goes back there and 'he remained
there'. He waits; he prepares himself for his last journey to
Jerusalem. In John's perspective, what occasions his final ascent
to the city is the call of Martha and Mary. John makes a very close
connection between the raising of Lazarus and the events of the
passion (see 11.45–53; 12.9–11) and, of course, it is the starting
point for Jesus' descent into the city in his Palm Sunday procession. In the account of John 11, Jesus leads his people into a
revolutionary new view of God on this mountain, requiring three
major shifts or transitions in their understanding.[3]

From God of gaps to God of glory

The chapter begins with Martha sending an urgent request to
Jesus: 'Lord, he whom you love is ill' (v. 3). This is pregnant with
the hope that Jesus will leave whatever he is doing and come and
heal Martha's brother immediately. Martha is focusing on the
presenting problem; she sees only illness, a brother who is sick.
She acknowledges Jesus to be 'Lord' but seems closed in her thinking about what might happen. She expects – demands – a miracle
of healing; she wants Jesus on her own terms; wants him as a
problem solver who can come in with his magic and mend the
situation. Martha experiences hurt and confusion when things
don't turn out as she imagined, and faces an agonizing wait as
Jesus deliberately delays his coming to Bethany.

Jesus is actually motivated by love and has a better gift in
store: 'though Jesus loved Martha and her sister and Lazarus,
after having heard that Lazarus was ill, he stayed two days longer
in the place where he was' (John 11.5–6). However, from Martha's
standpoint Jesus is being callous or inefficient, and she cannot
understand why he doesn't rush to her aid. Lazarus dies and is
laid in the tomb, but Martha sends no further requests to Jesus
– for her it has been a total failure, disaster, the end.

Jesus is very emphatic in his response to Martha's prayer: 'This
illness does not lead to death; rather it is for God's glory, so that

the Son of God may be glorified through it' (John 11.4). Again, outside Lazarus' tomb Jesus says to Martha, 'Did I not tell you that if you believed, you would see the glory of God?' (v. 40). What is 'glory' in John's perspective? It is the visible radiance of the divine presence – a sign that God is powerfully at work. John introduces this key theme in his words, 'And the Word became flesh and lived among us, and we have seen his glory, the glory as of a father's only son, full of grace and truth' (1.14). How is this glory to be revealed? God's glory is manifested through 'signs' like the transformation that took place at Cana (John 2.11). But it is supremely and paradoxically to be revealed on the cross. While other parts of the New Testament suggest that Jesus first suffers and then receives glory in the resurrection/ascension (Luke 24.26; Heb. 2.9), John alone sees the crucifixion of Christ as the greatest moment of glorification. In the fourth Gospel, Christ can say of his passion: 'The hour has come for the Son of Man to be glorified' (John 12.23; see also 7.39; 13.31; 17.1–5). Jesus approaches his death not as a disaster to be endured but as a glory to be embraced, for the cross is the moment of salvation. From the cross flows forgiveness and hope – it is the greatest hour of God's revelation, the laying bare of his presence.

Jesus, in the fourth Gospel, seems to be echoing Ezekiel's vision (11.22–24) of old. Immediately after his beautiful promise that God will give his people a new heart and a new spirit (a reading we have at the Easter Vigil), he sees the Shekinah glory of the Lord heading out of the city and hovering mysteriously over the Mount of Olives – it has left its captivity in the Holy of Holies in the Temple and is now moving across the land. No longer imprisoned within the confines of a 'holy place', the glory of God is now free to wander across the terrain and manifest itself in all sorts of places – the glory of God is on the loose!

Martha is invited to pray, not for Lazarus' healing but for the revelation of the glory of God. Do we, like her, have in fact too low an expectation of intercession, asking for restoration of a deteriorating situation when we could be asking for the revelation of the glory of God?[4] Martha asked for Lazarus' healing from illness; what she in fact goes on to receive, as Lazarus rises from the tomb, is the astounding vision of Christ as the vanquisher of death. Moreover she receives the salvation of the world; for, in John's view, Lazarus' rising precipitates and leads directly to the crucifixion. As a result of his rising, the Jews take counsel how to put Jesus to death.

In this first transition Martha has to let go of her small and narrow expectations and allow Christ to surprise her with the revelation of his glory, which is beyond her wildest imagination. As the Letter to the Ephesians puts it:

> Now to him who by the power at work within us is able to accomplish abundantly far more than all we can ask or imagine, to him be glory in the church and in Christ Jesus to all generations, forever and ever. Amen.   (Eph. 3.20–21)

Like Martha we need to learn to give up any well-meaning tiny-mindedness. We must not confine God or box him into our inherited and preconceived ideas. We need to be open to the glory of Christ however and whenever it is to be revealed, most likely in the places and people we would least expect to find it. We need too to make a transition from prescriptive, manipulative styles of intercession, which almost amount to a desire to control God ('Lord, he whom you love is ill; meet this need'), to risky, open kinds of petition ('Lord, come and reveal your glory!'). We need to remember that intercession is inseparable from self-offering: as we bring a situation to God we bring ourselves and place ourselves, once again, at God's disposal.

From God of might to God of tears

Martha wanted Jesus to come urgently to Bethany as a visitor and drop-in miracle-worker; to come into the situation, do the job and return to his ministry elsewhere. She wanted an efficient Jesus – a Jesus on her own terms – who would be like some kind of emergency doctor, sorting out a crisis but having no relationship with his patients. Once again she is astounded to discover a different Jesus – a Lord who desires to enter into the very depths of her pain. John tells us that Jesus deliberately waits outside the village, wishing for a private rendezvous with the two sisters (John 11.28–37). He wants to greet them as individuals and minister to their hurts: seeing their tears 'he was greatly disturbed in spirit and deeply moved' (John 11.33). The Greek conveys a sense of Jesus experiencing an inward groaning. John then puts it poignantly: 'Jesus began to weep' (v. 35). Arriving at the tomb Jesus is 'again greatly disturbed' (v. 38). He ministers to Martha in a way she could never have expected – not the wonder-worker who just passes through, Jesus comes to put his arms around the sisters in compassionate love, feeling their pain and confusion. Martha is released from a functionalist view of Jesus.

In the perspective of the Letter to the Hebrews, Jesus continues this ministry of compassion today and for all time from his place in heaven: 'For we do not have a high priest who is unable to sympathize with our weaknesses' (Heb. 4.15). Indeed, Christ in heaven is depicted as the understanding advocate who 'always lives to make intercession' (Heb. 7.25). Christ maintains an unbreakable solidarity with all who weep. He continues to share our tears. This is a key element of intercession – as we share our situation with him, inviting him to draw near, we give him permission to enter our pain and confusion. This requires vulnerability on our part. Turning from a bossy type of prayer to a receptive type, Martha allows Jesus to weep beside her. In the perspective of Hebrews, we join our faltering prayers with the unceasing prayer of Christ the high priest.

On the Mount of Olives we gain special insights into the nature of Jesus. We see into his heart; we glimpse his deepest longings. He does not stand on this mount like a mighty victor but as a weeping God. It is on this mount that he shed tears over the holy city, as Luke tells us: 'As he came near and saw the city, he wept over it, saying, "If you, even you, had only recognized on this day the things that make for peace!"' (19.41–42). In the Garden of Gethsemane Jesus will weep again as he faces his destiny. Here in John 11 his tears bespeak an unbreakable solidarity with grieving humanity.

From God of the end to God of the now

When Jesus promises that Lazarus will rise again, Martha confesses her faith in the general resurrection at the end of times. 'I know that he will rise again in the resurrection on the last day' (11.24). She has hope in a distant futuristic event – part of traditional Jewish faith. This tenet is of course the usual and accepted doctrine that the Mount of Olives will witness the final judgement and the resurrection of the dead on Doomsday – a belief, we have seen, that comes from the prophets Zechariah and Joel. Only on the far horizon of history will God act decisively and make all things new. With Jesus, the future is now. He summons Martha to revolutionize her hope: 'I am the resurrection and the life. Those who believe' in me, even though they die, will live' (John 11.25).[5] Jesus invites her to release her grip on dogmatic definitions and turns upside down the conservative traditional faith Martha expressed. He blows apart her inherited religious and respectable mindset, smashes into pieces the remoteness of her hope by declaring that the eschatological, end-time 'life of the world to come' is already, right now, breaking into people's lives. He dares her to step out of her cocoon of inherited faith and make the leap of faith into this new revelation, asking: 'Do you believe this?' (v. 26). Jesus, the resurrection and the life, stands on the very mountain which, with all its tombs, longs for the day of renewal. Martha is summoned to take the risk of trusting Jesus as the one who, even now, ushers in the new age.

This is of course a major theme in the Gospels. According to the Synoptics, Jesus inaugurates his ministry with the words: 'The time is fulfilled, and the kingdom of God has come near; repent, and believe in the good news.' In John's Gospel the time for God to act is *now*. 'Very truly, I tell you, the hour is coming, and is now here, when the dead will hear the voice of the Son of God, and those who hear will live' (5.25). Eternal life is not a faraway dream but a present possibility: 'this is eternal life, that they may know you, the only true God, and Jesus Christ whom you have sent' (17.3). This is realized eschatology – what we had seen as a distant and remote hope is happening in our very midst, wherever Jesus is allowed to be active. As Paul puts it, 'See, now is the acceptable time; see, now is the day of salvation!' (2 Cor. 6.2). Long ago the psalmist had put it: 'O that today you would listen to his voice!' (Ps. 95.7).

As Lazarus comes out of the tomb Jesus says 'Unbind him, and let him go' (John 11.44). This is a vivid image. It speaks of Jesus wanting to liberate us from all that confines us, including narrow religious ideas. Let us not restrict God to the narrow concepts we inherit, to our meagre hopes. Let us dare to trust him completely and lead us to new visions.

According to John the raising of Lazarus leads directly to the crucifixion, as we noted. Soon Jesus will lead his disciples and all who would follow to the crest of the hill to begin his Palm Sunday descent into the holy city, the city of his passion. As he does this, John tells us:

> So the crowd that had been with him when he called Lazarus out of the tomb and raised him from the dead continued to testify. It was also because they heard that he had performed this sign that the crowd went to meet him. The Pharisees then said to one another, 'You see, you can do nothing. Look, the world has gone after him!' (John 12.17–19)

We too must cross the threshold of the Mount of Olives, go after him and see what happens to us next.

Questions for reflection

1 How open are you to glimpsing the glory of God in situations of pain?
2 In our own lives, how can we sense what God is doing? Can we believe that the glory is just below the surface, ready to break out?
3 Notice again the shifts and transitions taking place in Martha and Mary. Which one can you identify most closely with?
4 Are there things we are procrastinating about, putting off to the future, like Martha and her distant hope in the resurrection? How can we embrace God's 'Now' and welcome him this very moment?
5 How do you think that this episode prepared the disciples for the events of the first Holy Week, which was soon to begin?

Prayer exercise

In a time of silence take the chance to work through the three transitions of this chapter, and ask yourself how they resonate with your own experience.

Reflect on how you go about intercessory prayer. What are you asking for when you pray? What image of God do you have in mind when you intercede? Dare you seek the healing presence of God right now?

Then end with these petitions, which express the transitions of the Mount of Olives.

> Lead us from narrowness of vision to new glimpses
>   of glory!
> Lead us from ideas of a remote God to Jesus as our
>   brother embracing us!
> Lead us from distant hopes to welcoming your grace
>   in our lives this very moment!

For further reading

D. Dales, *Glory! The Spiritual Theology of Michael Ramsey* (Norwich: Canterbury Press, 2003).

J. B. Philips, *Your God is too Small* (London: Epworth Press, 1961).

J. N. Ward, *The Use of Praying* (London: Epworth Press, 1967).

9

Passing over

--------•:•:•--------

'Christ our Passover has been sacrificed for us, therefore let us keep the feast'.[1] From the Hebrew *pesach* and the Greek *pascha* we get in English the word 'paschal', understanding the events of Christ's passion, death and resurrection in terms of a new Passover. As Ronald Rolheiser reminds us, Christian spirituality is essentially paschal in nature. He contrasts two kinds of death: terminal death, which ends possibilities; and paschal death, which opens us to deeper and richer life.[2] In this chapter we discover that the paschal mystery is very much bound up with the idea of crossing thresholds. Paul celebrates these transitions in his hymn about Christ's *kenosis*: 'he emptied himself . . . he humbled himself . . . God also highly exalted him' (Phil. 2.6–11). We will look here at four scenes in a drama that both captivates and liberates us.

The threshold of freedom

The very origin of the word Passover concerns the *limen* of the exodus. God's instruction to his people on the brink of their liberation from the captivity and slavery of Pharaoh is this:

> take a lamb for each family, a lamb for each household . . . the whole assembled congregation of Israel shall slaughter it at twilight. They shall take some of the blood and put it on the two doorposts and the lintel of the houses . . . The blood shall be a sign for you on the houses where you live: when I see the blood, I will pass over you, and no plague shall destroy you. (Exod. 12.3, 6–7, 13)

The very threshold of the house is marked by the blood of the lamb. This is the *limen*, the threshold of the journey to liberation, the starting line of the race to freedom, the brink of escape – blood on the wood.

Jesus gathers his friends for a final Passover together.[3] He understood his passion in terms of a new and final Passover. The disciples are expecting the usual elements, which include bread and wine, to be accompanied by the traditional *haggadah*, the words of interpretation. However, Jesus gives a stunningly alternative *haggadah* and thereby reveals what he thinks about his impending death. 'This cup, which you are expecting to recall the exodus, is my blood to be shed for you. This unleavened bread, which you are expecting to recall the eve of liberation, the night before the great escape to freedom, is my body to be broken for you.' Jesus is suggesting that the wood of the cross will become a new lintel, a new doorway to freedom, the *limen* of a new exodus into freedom, not from the tyranny of a pharaoh but from humanity's greatest enemies: death and sin. Blood on the wood – a new deliverance is at hand.

All the usual elements of the Passover are present at the Last Supper, according to the Gospel accounts – the bread, the cup, the dish (dipping sauce for bitter herbs), the closing hymn – but one thing is not mentioned, one thing is missing: there is no reference to the lamb itself. It seems that Jesus understands himself as the paschal lamb. The Baptist had greeted him at the very beginning as the 'lamb of God'. Jesus had earlier identified with the suffering servant of Isaiah, who spoke of the 'lamb that is led to the slaughter'. The scholar Joachim Jeremias puts it:

> With the words *deb bishri*, 'this is my (sacrificial) flesh', and *den idmi*, 'this is my (sacrificial) blood', Jesus is therefore most probably speaking of himself as the paschal lamb. He is *the eschatological paschal lamb*, representing the fulfilment of all that of which the Egyptian paschal lamb and all the subsequent sacrificial paschal lambs were the prototype.[4]

In his action at the table, which becomes the basis for the Christian Eucharist, he is inaugurating a new exodus, a new Passover, a new beginning for humanity. He is telling us that he sees the coming cross as making possible a new release from captivity and from the incarceration of death and sin.

Going to Gethsemane

Jesus does not go straight from the Last Supper to his crucifixion. He first has to enter the liminal place called Gethsemane (literally, 'the place of the oil press'). It is truly another *limen*, another threshold. Jesus must face human terrors and share in humanity's darkest fears. But he does not tread this path entirely alone. He longs to be accompanied. The story of Gethsemane is full of invitations to his disciples: 'Rise, let us be on our way' (John 14.31); 'remain here, and stay awake with me' (Matt. 26.38); 'Get up and pray' (Luke 22.46). And at the time of the arrest he says, 'Get up, let us be going' (Matt. 26.46). Jesus wants to take his best friends into the darkness with him. This gives new poignancy to his call, 'Follow me.' John's Gospel emphasizes this theme: 'Where I am, there you may be also' (John 14.3). He is emphatic: 'Whoever serves me must follow me, and where I am, there will my servant be also' (John 12.26). Jesus wants us to accompany him on this Gethsemane journey.

Luke describes Jesus as being in an *agonia* (22.44). This is the only time the word is used in the New Testament, and carries the meaning of an intense struggle for victory, wrestling, contest: Gethsemane becomes a battlefield with the powers of darkness. The word denotes both physical and spiritual suffering: 'he began to be distressed and agitated. And he said to them, "I am deeply grieved, even to death"' (Mark 14.33–34). Mark uses here three powerful verbs that take us into the heart of Christ's experience. *Ekthambeisthai* means he became utterly dismayed, tormented. It can also have the sense of being astonished, astounded. *Adeemonein* conveys the sense that he was seized by horror, gripped by a very intense anguish. *Perilupos* means he is grieved, exceedingly sorrowful, heartbroken, overcome with sadness. The heavy darkness presses Jesus into the dust of the ground. The soil is wet, not with the morning dew but with the tears of Christ: 'Jesus offered up prayers and supplications, with loud cries and tears, to the one who was able to save him from death' (Heb. 5.7). What is going on here, and how does it resonate with our prayer?

Jesus is standing in solidarity with all those who face their darkest hour. In this most human of scenes, Jesus is identifying with all those who through time will be crushed by their destiny and find themselves prostrate on the ground. But one fact is significant above all else: he brings his questions, doubts and fears to one he calls *Abba*; exposes his heart's anxieties to *Abba*. In the darkness of the garden he enters into an intimacy with the Father, and as a result Gethsemane becomes a threshold, a place of crossing. There seems to be a triple movement involved.

First, there is a passage from attachment to bereavement. A sense of loss – a rupturing of relationships – devastates Jesus. He had delighted in the intimate company of his disciples throughout his journeys and now, he senses, this is coming to an end. Now there is a loosening of the bonds of friendship, in one sense, a necessary detachment, for Jesus has to separate himself from even his closest disciples, and after the Easter mystery things will never be the same again. Jesus is alone. He experiences the dark depression of mourning – it is his 'grief work'. This is what Richard Foster calls 'the prayer of relinquishment'.[5] Letting go – resonating with the ancient experience of exodus and exile – is fundamental to Christian prayer. It lies at the heart of the matter. For ourselves, we need to let go of illusions, false concepts of God and self, attachments that have become less than health-giving. We need to enter the prayer of relinquishment in many different ways.

Second, Jesus transits from terror to trust, from agitation to composure. He comes close, humanly speaking, to falling to pieces, but moves to a fresh perspective and a renewed sense of his destiny. This enables him to face the onslaughts and attacks of the trials that night with an astonishing dignity and calm that he sustains throughout the long hours of his passion.

Third, Jesus makes a passage from resistance to surrender. Looking his impending death in the face, symbolized in taking a draught from the bitter cup, he prays: 'Abba, Father, for you all things are possible; remove this cup from me.' For a moment he is filled with a very human sense of dread in the face of suffering, but he is able to go on, 'yet, not what I want, but what you want' (Mark 14.36). Slowly yet deliberately and decisively, there is an abandonment to God, a yielding, a submission, a giving in, a movement from hesitant holding back to courageous self-emptying.

In our own experience of prayer, resistance takes many forms as we seek to duck out of what God is asking of us or avoid the closer encounter with God. In the great classic *Self-Abandonment to Divine Providence*, Jean-Pierre de Caussade (1675–1751) encourages us to abide in a state of surrender to God.[6] De Caussade urged his readers to strive for a synergy, an active co-operation with God's will: 'We know that in all things God works for good for those who love God, who are called according to his purpose.'[7] De Caussade believed that God is supremely active in the world, guiding all things according to his divine plans. Our part is to be awake and responsive to God's actions, to allow him to move and direct our life in the midst of change. We are to train ourselves to recognize God's hand of providence in the 'chances and changes of this mortal life'.

De Caussade gave us the striking phrase, 'the sacrament of the present moment'. He teaches us that we should not live in the past nor become anxious about the future, but rather be totally available to God this day and this very moment: 'See, now is the acceptable time; see, now is the day of salvation' (2 Cor. 6.2). Today, right now, God waits to meet us. De Caussade urges us to live in an attitude of continual surrender to God, yielding ourselves totally to him without qualification or preconditions, so we can become channels through which he can work: 'Loving, we wish to be the instrument of his action so that his love can operate in and through us.'[8] We are to live by humble trust in God, confident that he is working his purposes out. We are not to seek our own fulfilment but God's kingdom: 'Follow your path without a map, not knowing the way, and all will be revealed to you. Seek only God's kingdom and his justice through love and obedience, and all will be granted to you.'[9] Abandoned into God's hands, we are to 'go with the flow' as he opens and closes doors before us.

But what if our prayer resembles Gethsemane, and suffering and upheavals come our way – can these be welcomed as God's will for us? Should we not try to fight against them? De Caussade warns that we must not set bounds or limits to God's plans. He is a 'God of surprises'. He works in unpredictable and unlikely ways and we should be ready for anything: 'The terrifying objects put in our way are nothing. They are only summoned to embellish our lives with glorious adventures.'[10] Hardships can be in God's hands pathways to growth: 'With God, the more we seem to loose, the more we gain. The more he takes from us materially, the more he gives spiritually.'[11] We should not resent difficult circumstances but rather listen to what God is saying to us through them.

How then is it possible to cultivate an attitude of such openness to God? De Caussade affirms that it is achieved by living in communion with God and allowing Jesus Christ to dwell at the very centre of our being. The Christ who longs to live within us is 'noble, loving, free, serene, and fearless'.[12] De Caussade has a vision of the Christ-life growing within each person who has the courage to surrender to him. This is the secret of recognizing 'the sacrament of the present moment'.

Jesus emerges from Gethsemane a changed man. He is able to face the coming humiliations with astonishing gracefulness. In John's Gospel he even seems to take charge of the situation.[13]

Standing on Calvary

Christ's journey to the cross, the *via dolorosa*, has a momentum and dynamic whereby we are caught up into the flow of his self-offering – we can't hold back. Like some kind of magnetic river it draws us in. We join Simon of Cyrene, Veronica and the others in the unstoppable movement towards the hill of Calvary, and we find it to be a journey towards the total oblation of ourselves in and through Christ. 'Jesus also suffered outside the city gate ... Let us then go to him outside the camp' (Heb. 13.12–13). With his arms outstretched on the cross, Jesus invites us to step into the liminal space of Calvary. It is truly the *limen* of our salvation; it is betwixt and between. The cross stretches vertically as a bridge between heaven and earth. Its horizontal arm points to the criminals crucified to left and right, symbols of the world's complex need. The arms of Christ beckon and summon us and long to enfold us unconditionally. Into this space, first step Mary and the Beloved Disciple – their relationship is about to be changed forever. Jesus says to the disciple, 'Here is your mother.' To Mary he says, 'Woman, here is your son.' And, the author notes, 'from that hour the disciple took her into his own home' (John 19.26–27). Victor Turner has observed that in liminal spaces relationships are reordered as *communitas* is born. This is happening on Calvary.[14] Jesus is gathering together and reshaping lives. A new family, the core of the Church, comes into being. Diverse ages and backgrounds are brought together. According to Matthew's Gospel, John's natural mother is also standing near the cross. Regular, normal, biological relationships are shaken up – new spiritual relations are established. The new community is to be energized by reciprocal and costly love and care, as symbolized by the embrace of Mary and John.

The new community created at the cross is formed too by the flow of forgiveness. The words resound from the gibbet: 'Father, forgive!' (Luke 23.34). Mary and John are not the only members of this community – they are joined by three figures who represent the outcast and the untouchable. Embraced within the liminal space of the cross is the so-called 'repentant thief'. This guy is a political activist who comes from the fringes of society, and stands for the oppressed who protest against the status quo. He will enter paradise by his act of faith. Close by is a figure representing the political and military establishment: the Roman centurion, who finds himself confessing: 'Truly, this was God's Son!' With them, of course, stands Mary Magdalene, the wounded/healed lover, who will become the first witness of the resurrection. It is astonishing to see who are the founder-members of the new community: a despairing mother; a fisherman disciple; a political guerrilla; a soldier who stands for the might of Rome; one who loves much, because she is forgiven much. The liminal space of Calvary has a place for all. The cross is a place of reconciliation, and the outstretched arms of Jesus encompass the world. There is room for us too to stand in the transformative, liminal space of Calvary.

Entering the tomb

The body of Jesus is buried and the tomb sealed. On Holy Saturday there descends on the disciples a numbness, a sense of disbelief, a sense that nothing is happening, that it is all over. There is a lingering darkness and gloom; an unspeakable sense of loss and the burning question: 'How could it all have ended like this?'

Yet in Christian tradition God has a habit of working in the darkness. The Apostles' Creed affirms: 'He descended into hell.' In the mystery of Holy Saturday the work of redemption is being accomplished silently, secretly, in the darkness of the grave. Christ is busy in the underworld: Christ 'was put to death in the flesh, but made alive in the spirit, in which also he went and made a proclamation to the spirits in prison' (1 Peter 3.18–19). The Orthodox icon of the descent into hell, as we recalled, depicts a radiant Christ pulling up Adam and Eve, by their hands, from their graves. Representing all humanity, they are being led into freedom, while death itself lies chained, bound and impotent.

Holy Saturday is a liminal space in which God is working in unfathomable ways. It resonates with prayer that finds itself in a dark place. John of the Cross spoke of the 'dark night of the soul' but understood this to be a positive and sometimes needful experience. John identifies three blessings of the dark night. First, in the dark we cannot actually see. Normally our senses are alert to all the sensory perceptions around us, and this can dissipate the soul. To pray in the darkness is to quieten our senses and wait for a deeper encounter with God, which lies beneath the surface. Second, in the dark we can't make out obstacles or turnings along the path, or sense the way clearly. So in prayer we must be prepared to venture into undiscovered, unfamiliar terrain, along pathways we have yet to tread. Third, the darkness can also represent the times we think we cannot pray, when we can't find the words and when we don't feel anything towards God, perhaps when we are spiritually confused. John assures us that abiding in the darkness of God can be authentic prayer. In the darkness we can make the greatest discoveries of God.

Holy Saturday becomes a day of deepest yearning and long-ing – the prayer of waiting. As Paul put it in Romans 8, 'the creation waits with eager longing for the revealing of the children of God . . . the creation itself will be set free from its bondage to decay and will obtain the freedom of the glory of the children of God' (vv. 19, 21). The tomb of prayer becomes the womb: 'the whole creation has been groaning in labour pains until now . . . [we] groan inwardly while we wait for adoption, the redemption of our bodies' (vv. 22–23). Paul assures us that while we find ourselves in this night of longing 'we do not know how to pray as we ought, but that very Spirit intercedes with sighs too deep for words' (v. 26).

Sometimes it is necessary to wait in the darkness of prayer. The darkness resonates with a process of radical dispossession that John of the Cross sees at the heart of prayer's movement from egocentricity to God-centredness, a process in which God seeks to reshape us and convert the ego. The renunciation of one's own confidences enables a total surrender to God – the pain to be faced is that of being stripped of our egotistical powers. As John Follent puts it:

> The abandonment of self-mastery and the taking on of a radical dependence on God will necessarily be accompanied by a sense of being undone or being annihilated, yet such an anxiety is quite ungrounded. In fact, the discovery that one can no longer find one's guarantees in oneself may indeed be a sign that progress in the life with God is finally being achieved.[15]

It is in the darkness of this liminal space that we are undone and remade. We discover the meaning of Christ's words:

> unless a grain of wheat falls into the earth and dies, it remains just a single grain; but if it dies, it bears much fruit. Those who love their life lose it, and those who hate their life in this world will keep it for eternal life.   (John 12.24–25)

At the heart of Christian prayer the central experience is to par-ticipate in the paschal mystery. This is not something we just celebrate each Easter – we need to live it daily. Paul has striking phrases: 'with Christ I hang on the cross'.[16] As the NRSV puts it: 'I have been crucified with Christ; and it is no longer I who live, but it is Christ who lives in me' (Gal. 2.19–20). Paul tells us that in baptism we are buried and raised with Christ:

> When we were baptized into his death, we were placed into the tomb with him. As Christ was brought back from death to life by the glorious power of the Father, so we, too, should live a new kind of life.[17]   (Rom. 6.4)

In the prayer of Holy Saturday, we allow God to kill off the old self (Rom. 6.6). There is a drowning to be accomplished – the old life is to be asphyxiated. This is the most fundamental letting go. But Paul is reassuring: 'if we have died with Christ, we believe that we will also live with him' (Rom. 6.8).

Questions for reflection

1 A question from the Last Supper: How can you participate in the Eucharist so it becomes a meal of your liberation?
2 A question from Gethsemane: What do you need to let go of in order to move forward spiritually?
3 A question from Calvary: How does your experience of the cross affect your relationships?
4 A question from the tomb: What needs to die in you, so you become more fully alive in Christ?
5 In what ways, do you think, can you live out the Easter mystery daily?

Prayer exercise

Enter one of the four liminal spaces considered in this chapter and see what happens. Choose one of the scenes and visualize it in your imagination. For example, in the upper room, take your place beside the disciples at the table and watch what unfolds. In the Garden of Gethsemane, picture the overhanging olive trees and the wet grass and join Peter, James and John in their sleepiness and watchfulness. Observe Jesus and listen in again to his prayer. At the foot of the cross join those who are forming the new *communitas*. Stand with Mary and John, with the centurion and the women. Look up at the face of Jesus. See his outstretched hands longing to enfold. At the tomb, join with Mary Magdalene in her tears and joy. In each of the scenes picture yourself in closest proximity to Jesus. Lower your defences. Ask the Holy Spirit to come to aid you. As you see the story unfold once more, notice what reactions are taking place in you. Note them down in a journal. What transition, shift or movement do you sense you being called to?

For further reading

C. Chapman, *Seeing in the Dark: Pastoral Perspectives on Suffering from the Christian Spiritual Tradition* (Norwich: Canterbury Press, 2013).

I. Matthew, *The Impact of God: Soundings from St John of the Cross* (London: Hodder & Stoughton, 1995).

10

Reaching beyond limits

Mark's Gospel has the most enigmatic ending – the risen Christ does not appear in the Gospel at all. Instead, coming to the tomb to anoint the dead body of Jesus and pay their last respects, Mary Magdalene and her companions are surprised by the sight of a young man dressed in white – an angel? He has an unexpected message: 'You are looking for Jesus of Nazareth, who was crucified. He has been raised; he is not here. Look, there is the place they laid him.' He goes on: 'But go, tell his disciples and Peter that he is going ahead of you to Galilee; there you will see him, just as he told you' (Mark 16.6–7). Jesus will not be found in Jerusalem, the religious capital, the centre of the religious establishment, where the divine presence was expected to be located. Rather, the risen Christ is to be discovered in remote Galilee, the place on the periphery, the margins – '*there* you will see him'. The young man reminds the women that this is precisely what Jesus had said himself. As Jesus had taken his disciples to Gethsemane on the Mount of Olives on the eve of his passion, he had indeed said, 'But after I am raised up, I will go before you to Galilee' (Mark 14.28). In Matthew's Gospel there is a double emphasis on this point – the words of the angel are repeated, then Jesus appears, but only for a fleeting moment. He has one message: 'go and tell my brothers to go to Galilee; there they will see me' (Matt. 28.10).

So what is the significance of Jesus' longing to reveal himself not at the centre of things but on the margins? We realize that Galilee itself is a liminal place and that Christ waits to meet us in such places. Matthew's Gospel had quoted Isaiah 9.1–2 at the very start of this account of the ministry, to show the context chosen by Jesus: 'Land of Zebulun, land of Naphtali, on the road by the sea, across the Jordan, Galilee of the Gentiles – the people who sat in darkness have seen a great light' (Matt. 4.15). On what grounds does Galilee acquire this designation 'Galilee of the Gentiles'? Is it a compliment or an insult? The phrase means literally 'circle of pagans'. Indeed, it is likely that the Galilee region was much more mixed in terms of Jewish and Gentile populations than other regions of the land. A semi-autonomous frontier region, it was exposed to the nearby foreign countries and ethnicities. Studies by Richard Horsley and Sean Freyne have illuminated for us the marginality of Galilee.[1] Freyne calls Galilee 'a symbol of the periphery becoming the new non-localized centre of divine presence'.[2] It maintained both a physical distance from the Temple on Zion and an ideological distance, prepared to make a critique of the self-serving Jerusalem clerical elite and their practices. It found itself on the edges. Galileans were mocked for their local accent – recall the girl's recognition of Peter's rough Aramaic tongue (Mark 14.70) – they were jeered at and scapegoated. 'Can anything good come out of Nazareth?' asks Nathaniel (John 1.46). 'Search and you will see that no prophet is to arise from Galilee' (John 7.52). It has been said:

> Galileans were not just left alone in their liminal situation but were oppressed, dehumanized and looked down upon. Galileans were marginalized by foreign invaders and also by the Jerusalem Temple-state . . . Galilee was repeatedly invaded and exploited by foreign empires throughout its history.[3]

But above all it was a place of deep poverty and need. The Galileans were crippled by heavy taxes, dues were owed to the Roman occupier, and Temple taxes added to the burden. At the time of Jesus, ordinary families were being forced to quit their ancestral landholdings where they had lived for centuries, in order to meet these demands. Land was also confiscated for the building projects and villas of the urban elite at Sepphoris and Tiberias. But then they had to pay rent for what had been their fields and homes – they became caught in a downwards economic spiral, tenants in their own property. We should note how many of Jesus' parables speak of absentee landlords who impose severe dues on their tenants (see, for example, Luke 16.1–8; Matt. 25.14–30). Tax and rent robbed the Galilean peasant farmer of two-thirds of the family income. Many were living at barely subsistence level.

No doubt Matthew preserves an original aspect of the Lord's Prayer when he puts it, 'forgive us our debts, as we also have forgiven our debtors' (Matt. 6.12). Jesus asks his disciples to pray for the coming of God's kingdom – a subversive prayer when taught and uttered in the context of first-century Galilee, for it embodies a challenge to the prevailing kingdom, the kingdom of Rome, the rule of the Caesar. But this imperial reign had become stiflingly oppressive for the Galileans. The area of Galilee became a base for resistance to Rome's occupation and perhaps the seedbed of the Zealot movement. The Gospels mention several times the designation *lestes* (for example, Mark 14.48; 15.27). Often translated 'thieves', this really denotes social bandits. Josephus tells us about revolutionary activists in Galilee who sought to undermine Roman domination by acts of sabotage or terrorism – the precursors of the Jewish Zealots and Sicarri. Where there is oppression amid powerlessness, one reaction is the rise of violent terrorists or guerrilla fighters. Ever since the uprising by Judas the Galilean in 4 BC, Galilee was infamous for these protesters and rebels.

'I will go before you to Galilee, there you will see me' – can we now realize what these words mean?

> I will meet you in the liminal place, the land that is betwixt and between, caught between foreign countries and the religious centre; a place of oppression and protest. I will meet you in the places that need healing and encouragement. No need to look for me in the corridors of power or at the religious centre. I will be found among the poor, the broken and hurting. Find me among the rejected and stigmatized. I wait for you in situations of injustice and dehumanization. *There* I will meet you.

This should not be a surprise to us for we recall Christ's parable:

> Then the king will say to those at his right hand, 'Come, you that are blessed by my Father, inherit the kingdom prepared for you from the foundation of the world; for I was hungry

and you gave me food, I was thirsty and you gave me something to drink, I was a stranger and you welcomed me, I was naked and you gave me clothing, I was sick and you took care of me, I was in prison and you visited me.' And the king will answer them, 'Truly I tell you, just as you did it to one of the least of these who are members of my family, you did it to me.' (Matt. 25.34–36, 40)

The risen Christ, bounding across Galilean hills, summons us to make three transitions in our life:

Move from the centre to the edge

In order to go to the margins, we have to leave the centre, where we often feel the need to be. As Pedro Casaldáliga and José María Vigil put it:

> We live the option for the poor first as a break with the attitudes of the dominant classes, which we have usually absorbed . . . with the mind-set of those who dominate society . . . This is a departure from our own class, a difficult sacrifice, a kenosis . . . After this break, the option for the poor leads us to an exodus, makes us go out and meet the other person, go to the poor quarters of town, enter the world of the poor and accept it as our own. It is an incarnation, an identification with the world of the poor.[4]

We think of how Christ got alongside the crushed and the wounded. As we follow Jesus to Galilee we recall his manifesto declared to the people of Nazareth, taken from Isaiah 61:

> The Spirit of the Lord is upon me,
>> because he has anointed me
>>> to bring good news to the poor.
> He has sent me to proclaim release to the captives
>> and recovery of sight to the blind,
>>> to let the oppressed go free,
> to proclaim the year of the Lord's favour.
>> (Luke 4.18–19)

The disciples were to report back to the Baptist what they had witnessed going on in Galilee: 'Go and tell John what you have seen and heard: the blind receive their sight, the lame walk, the lepers are cleansed, the deaf hear, the dead are raised, the poor have good news brought to them' (Luke 7.22). To follow Jesus to Galilee demands that we linger on the edge of the Church, alert and responsive to those who are just beginning their spiritual quest. And it demands that we position ourselves on the edge of society, on the fringes, among the confused and searching.

Turn from the self to the neighbour

Liberation theologians rightly call this a 'conversion to the neighbour'. Gustavo Gutiérrez tells us:

> A spirituality of liberation will centre on a conversion to the neighbour, the oppressed person, the exploited social class, the despised ethnic group, the dominated country . . . Conversion means a radical transformation of ourselves; it means thinking, feeling and living as Christ – present in exploited and alienated persons. To be converted is to commit oneself to the process of the liberation of the poor and oppressed, to commit oneself lucidly, realistically, and concretely.[5]

It requires of us that *metanoia* we considered in Chapter 3: going beyond the existing mindset or into a wider one. We see a vivid example of this in the story of St Francis of Assisi. In 1226 he wrote in his heartfelt *Testament*:

> The Lord gave me, Brother Francis, thus to begin doing penance in this way: for when I was in sin, it seemed too bitter for me to see lepers. And the Lord himself led me among them and I showed mercy to them. And when I left them, what had seemed bitter to me was turned into sweetness of soul and body.[6]

Francis had to overcome physical nausea and spiritual revulsion in order to find the crucified and risen Christ in the disfigured features of those suffering from leprosy. Once, after kissing a leper, Francis asked himself: 'Was that Jesus I just embraced?'

Shift from the routine to the unexpected

Routinely, Christians meet their Lord in broken bread and poured-out wine. What is needed is that we then search out his real presence in the lives of the poor. The Bishop of Zanzibar put it memorably in his 1923 address, 'Your Present Duty'. He spoke of the joy of encountering the risen Christ in the Eucharist, but this was to be a beginning not an ending of the quest for the risen Lord:

> Now go out into the highways and hedges . . . Go out and look for Jesus in the ragged, in the naked, in the oppressed and sweated [*sic*], in those who have lost hope, in those who are struggling to make good. Look for Jesus. And when you see him, gird yourselves with his towel and try to wash their feet.[7]

The dying and rising Christ shows up unexpected and uninvited. He surprises with his presence. He turns up, it seems, when people are making transitions. There he comes, out of the blue, on the road to Emmaus. Drawing alongside the two walking away from Jerusalem, he leads them into a new future. He appears to Saul as he travels on the road to Damascus and turns his life upside down. Later, Paul tells us that the risen Christ appeared to 500 people at one time (1 Cor. 15.6). We must refuse to limit the power of the resurrection – resurrection can break out in the most unlikely places. Do not attempt to predict where the risen Christ will emerge next. Paul talked about the foolishness of God unseating conventional wisdom; he talked about the folly of the cross and the craziness of the resurrection (1 Cor. 1.18–31).

An unfettered Jesus, bursting from the tomb, goes ahead to 'Galilee' (Mark 16.7). Jesus is on the loose; he cannot be held down! He opens new futures for us. As Leonardo Boff puts it:

> The resurrection is a process that began with Jesus and will go on until it embraces all creation. Wherever an authentically

human life is growing in the world, wherever justice is triumphing over the instincts of domination, wherever grace is winning out over the power of sin . . . wherever hope is resisting the lure of cynicism or despair, there the process of resurrection is being turned into a reality.[8]

Peter had returned to Galilee after the first Easter, as directed. But he went back to his old occupation of fishing (John 21.3). Perhaps he thought the adventure was over, completed. He had been on quite a journey: Jesus had led him and the disciples over the hills to the Mediterranean coast; across the lake, into the desert, through Samaria's valleys; up mountains – he would never be the same again. But standing at the liminal shoreline of the Sea of Galilee, the risen Christ says to Peter, 'Follow me!' (John 21.22). Peter had first heard those words three years earlier when he was a contented fisherman, quite settled into his way of life. He must have quaked when he heard this summons repeated to him – he began to realize that the adventure had only just begun!

'Follow me!' The words resound across the centuries and reach our own ears today. Get yourself ready for adventures. Pray for an intrepid heart. Be ready for more travels. Dare to be venturesome. Jesus wants to lead you beyond where you are right now. He wants to lead you over the edge.

'I will go ahead of you to Galilee.' Jesus awaits us in the Galilee-like populations of our own time. He is already there – he does not need to be brought there. He is there, and we will always be catching up with him. He, indeed, is the forerunner, the pioneer, the precursor – he gets there before we do. But he waits for us to greet him and honour him in the poor and marginalized and to recognize his features in the faces of those who suffer. In the Gospels the risen Christ instructs us to go beyond borders and reach across frontiers. Matthew's Gospel ends with the Great Commission: 'Go therefore and make disciples of all nations' (28.19). The Greek *ethnos* denotes nations or different peoples. We are to get ourselves across the boundaries, over frontiers. But we are not alone in the venture: 'remember, I am with you always, to the end of the age' (Matt. 28.20).

Luke gives us a similar charge from the risen Christ: 'you will receive power when the Holy Spirit has come upon you; and you will be my witnesses in Jerusalem, in all Judea and Samaria, and to the ends of the earth' (Acts 1.8). The apostles are not only to go into despised Samaria but into every region on the planet. There are no longer any no-go areas, actual or metaphorical. There are no limits. We are to go beyond the edge, with Jesus. It is in crossing into the uncertain liminal places that we will encounter the risen Lord.

Questions for reflection

1 What is 'Galilee' in your context? Who are the marginalized and stigmatized, and where are they?
2 How will you get to meet them?
3 Who or where is the most unexpected person or place where you have encountered the risen Christ?
4 Why is conversion to the neighbour an integral transition in our ongoing conversion?
5 'Linger on the edge of the Church.' What does this look like in your own situation?

Prayer exercise

Use the 'cross-prayers' devised by Francis of Assisi. Open your arms wide – extend them as far as you can. This is first to embody a solidarity with the cross. Think of Jesus opening wide his arms on the cross to embrace all who suffer, all who are in any form of distress. Think of Christ's all-encompassing love and acceptance. Second, think of the risen Christ and the way he longs to enfold the whole of creation, the little ones and marginalized ones of the earth. Third, offer this prayer as an act of intercession. It is a prayer that hurts – in the sense that your arms will grow weary and ache. Moses prayed like this and had to have others hold up his arms (Exod. 17.11–12). As you feel the ache, let it connect you to those who are in pain, those who are hurting – the sick, the dispossessed, those whose human rights are trampled on. Finally, use this prayer-action as an act of self-offering. Offer yourself afresh to God for the part he has in store for you in his mission to the world.

For further reading

V. Elizondo, *A God of Incredible Surprises: Jesus of Galilee* (Oxford: Rowman & Littlefield, 2003).

A. D. Mayes, *Holy Land? Challenging Questions from the Biblical Landscape* (London: SPCK, 2011).

A. J. Roxburgh, *The Missionary Congregation, Leadership and Liminality* (Harrisburg, PA: Trinity Press International, 1997).

Appendix
Models of spiritual direction and accompaniment

―――♦♦♦―――

1 Wading across the river: priests and precursors

Two images of the spiritual director emerge from the transitions of the Jordan, and both are dripping wet! From the account of Joshua's crossing of the Jordan (Josh. 3) we get a dramatic image in the figures of the priests who stand in the place of risk and danger, stepping out to the swirling currents of the Jordan in front of God's people. They bear the Ark of the Covenant. They carry the sacred symbol of God's will. They are bearers of the sacred, the Holy; the Scripture, the divine Commandment. They carry with them the very power of God. And they are asked to tread first into the racing waters. They are required to be people of faith – big faith – for they believe the waters will cease when they place their feet in the torrent.[1]

We need spiritual directors and soul friends who will take God's people across thresholds, beyond boundaries, into uncharted waters, into unexplored lands. In that first crossing of the Jordan it is the priests who play such a crucial role, prepared to pave the way, trailblazers who dare to go first. Such priests are prepared for risk-taking, ready to lead their people from the front – and yet they also bring up the rear, for they will not leave the waters until the last person has crossed. This gives us our first vivid image and symbol of those called to be spiritual directors, who not only walk beside the person they are accompanying on the spiritual journey but also, at times, might need to walk before them and lead the way across the choppy waters. They need to be alert to 'landmarks' on the spiritual journey – indicators or signs of readiness for spiritual growth or the identification of barriers that impede growth. What are the clues and cues that suggest that this person is ready to cross the river?

A second image suggests itself to us from the account of Jesus' baptism: John the Baptist himself. John is waiting in the waters for the arrival of Jesus. John is the one who makes Christ's transition possible – the key facilitator, if you like. He welcomes Jesus into the swirling currents and stands by him. But while fulfilling an important role, he is conscious that he is an unworthy servant, not worthy to unloose the sandals of Jesus (Luke 3.16). He will say, 'He must increase, but I must decrease' (John 3.30). John knows he is both vital and insignificant. He will describe himself as 'the friend of the bridegroom, who stands and hears him, rejoices greatly at the bridegroom's voice' (John 3.29).

John indeed has a vital role to fulfil in relation to God's people. In the imagery of Isaiah 40, which is his key text, he must help to prepare hearts for God's advent, to clear the road, to help remove roadblocks and obstacles that might impede the encounter with God. John is also responsive to the different needs he encounters. He faces quite diverse groups – multitudes, tax collectors, soldiers – and has a unique word of counsel for each of them (Luke 3.10–14). Above all, John models the radical life. He dares to go first into the desert and wait in the silence. His greatest longing is that others will make the crossing through the mighty Jordan and enter into the blessings of the kingdom.

- How does the image of Joshua's priests in the Jordan challenge your view of spiritual direction?
- What does the image of John the Baptist say to your ministry of helping to facilitate spiritual transitions?

2 Advancing through desert margins: spiritual parents

We are called to support one another in the desert of prayer. Four things flow from this vocation of the desert parent, the *pneumatikos pater*.[2]

First the desert fathers and mothers were non-judgemental and accepting spiritual parents. They offered a spiritual nurture and care, with what we call these days 'tough love'. They called a spade a spade but they did not pass judgement on the seeker because they knew too well how fragile and weak they were themselves. So they were very compassionate. Don't take yourselves too seriously. Lighten up – some humour is good for the soul.

Second, they did emphasize that seekers must not seek any easy blessing but rather take responsibility for themselves, before God, and enter the way of repentance.

Third, the holy man or woman models the ascetic life, giving example to enquirers of patterns of holiness and purity of heart.

Fourth, the holy person gives advice, teaching or instruction to enquirers in response to their oft-repeated request, 'Give me a word, Father.' Such words of counsel, often pithy and enigmatic, were designed to uncover the heart's true desire rather than be directive in the sense of advice-giving.

The practice and ideal of spiritual parenthood, and the disciplines commended for spiritual development, were developed by several key ascetic leaders through the use of concepts that were to prove influential in the later tradition. John Cassian (365–435) helped to communicate the ideals of monastic direction to the West. After his own experience as a monk in Bethlehem and Egypt he travelled to Marseilles and the region of Provence, where he sought to put into practice what he had discovered in the desert. He wrote *Institutes* as a book for beginners and the *Conferences* as a study of the Egyptian ideal of the monk – both were to be greatly influential in the West, and Benedict acknowledges his debt to them at the end of his *Rule*. The *Conferences* present themselves as interviews with the holy men. As Kenneth Leech claims, 'The tradition of conferences, or extended discourse on spiritual problems, dates from the Rule of Pachomius, and by the end of the fourth century it was the standard method of spiritual direction.'[3]

Two themes in Cassian resonate with the double movement of exposure and enclosure.

Exposure needs the support of discernment (*diakrisis*)

In his sketches of the practice of spiritual fatherhood, Cassian called discernment 'the source and root of all the virtues'.[4] He places on Anthony's lips this definition:

> It keeps him [the monk] from veering to the right, that is, it keeps him from going with stupid presumption and excessive fervour beyond the boundary of reasonable restraint. It keeps him from going to the left to carelessness and sin, to sluggishness of spirit, and all this on the pretext of actually keeping the body under control.[5]

For Cassian, discernment, which can also be translated 'discretion', is a watchfulness and vigilance for the angelic and the demonic, a wariness of excess in physical deprivation and a healthy, compassionate account of humanity's weaknesses – in short, it stops ascetic practice from becoming dehumanizing and self-destructive. He advocates this as a guiding principle in the process we now call spiritual direction.

Enclosure leads to singleness of heart

Cassian advocates a clear vision, a singleness of purpose, in relation to the spiritual life:

> Every art and every discipline has a particular objective, that is to say, a target and an end particularly its own . . . the aim of our profession is the kingdom of God or the kingdom of heaven. But the point of reference, our objective, is a clean heart, without which it is impossible for anyone to reach our target.[6]

In such passages Cassian celebrates the heart as the centre of his anthropology – the meeting point or battleground of vices and virtues, an inner space that needs to be kept clear of disturbances so that it becomes ready for the contemplation (*theoria*) of God.

- How can the image of the director as spiritual father or mother be rescued from sounding too paternalistic or maternalistic?
- How responsible do you feel for the nurture and growth of the person you are directing?

3 Venturing to the coastlands: yapping dog

The image of a spiritual director suggested by the story of the Syrophoenician woman is that of the yapping hungry dog under the table. The woman points out that the dogs or puppies need to be noticed and responded to. They point to other voices that claim attention: spiritualities or traditions that have been ignored or are out of sight; the voices of the poor, dispossessed. The yelps of the puppies represent questions that do not go away; that cannot easily be dismissed or shrugged off; cries that cannot be silenced. Sometimes the spiritual director will need to be a nuisance, an irritant, like a dog that persistently nips the heels of the sitter, barking at times, interrupting self-preoccupation. Sometimes the director needs to show teeth! If there are signs that the person is descending into a narrow individualistic spirituality, then is the time to nip. In the story, Jesus is glad the woman notices the needs of the dogs, saying, 'great is your faith!' (Matt. 15.28). The spiritual director acts as a catalyst, triggering off fresh explorations of spirituality.

- How comfortable are you with the idea of the spiritual director as an irritant?
- What sources of spirituality unsettle you?

4 Traversing the risky lake: navigator

Paul lists as one of the gifts of the Spirit *kubernetes*. Lamely translated 'administration' (RSV), it means 'navigation' or 'helmsmanship' (1 Cor. 12.28). For Paul, the art of discerning the Spirit's movement, the art of recognizing the need of the moment, is akin to the skill of the ship's pilot and steersman who, working collaboratively alongside the captain, coxswain and the entire crew, will guide the ship in its adventures. In the seventh century John Climacus of Sinai speaks of the need for courageous spiritual directors using this image: 'A ship with a good navigator comes safely to port, God willing.'[7]

Our spiritual experience, especially when facing our demons or shadow side, can accurately be likened to traversing a stormy lake. The spiritual director will have two principal roles in this time of turbulence. He or she will first of all know how to read the climate of the soul being directed – whether it is time to hoist the sails, labour with oars or drift along with the wind of the Spirit. Jesus spoke of reading the signs of weather:

> He also said to the crowds, 'When you see a cloud rising in the west, you immediately say, "It is going to rain"; and so it happens. And when you see the south wind blowing, you say, "There will be scorching heat"; and it happens. You hypocrites! You know how to interpret the appearance of earth and sky, but why do you not know how to interpret the present time?' (Luke 12.54–56)

We need to have the sensitivity, alertness and courage to read what is going on in the other person: whether they are ready to move ahead and embrace their shadow, for example, or whether it is time to hang back.

The second role of the director in such circumstances is to be a figure of reassurance amid the storm. We think of the image of Jesus asleep on a pillow while the violent weather rages on (Mark 4.38), a picture of constancy, stability and perfect trust in God's providence. The person facing upheaval needs to hear our words that affirm that all is OK.

- What is your own experience of facing the storm of prayer?
- Who or what guided you through this experience, and how might it help you in supporting others?

5 Penetrating Samaria's border: thirsty pilgrim

The whole story of John 4 reads like a case study in spiritual direction. Jesus' dialogue embodies a model of direction. He is present as a weary and needy fellow-traveller. Eight things stand out.

1 Jesus situates himself *beside* the woman. He does not stand over against her but rather the account is vivid and emphatic: 'Jesus, tired out by his journey, was *sitting* by the well' (v. 6). He is on the same level as her, and looking yearningly into the ancient well, symbol of humanity's spiritual longing. Jesus is present to the woman as a pilgrim who is himself thirsting.

2 Jesus speaks with directness. There is no beating about the bush, rather clarity and precision: 'Give me a drink'; 'If you knew the gift of God' (v. 10).

3 Jesus affirms the woman as someone worthy of bearing the living water of the Spirit. However much traditional village values might ostracize her or the disciples reject her (v. 27), Jesus emphatically declares that she has the capacity to discover an inner spring of the Spirit.

4 Jesus allows her to ask questions. He does not quench her curiosity or questioning spirit. Three questions immediately bubble up from her: 'How is it . . .?' (v. 9); 'Where do you get . . .?' (v. 11); 'Are you greater . . .?' (v. 12). Jesus has created a climate of trust where she is comfortable in sharing her questions, which come straight from her soul.

5 Jesus challenges her. He challenges her over the issue of relationships (vv. 4, 16–18). He challenges her over her view about where one should worship (v. 21). 'You worship what you do not know' (v. 22).

6 Jesus speaks the truth: 'you have had five husbands, and the one you have now is not your husband' (v. 18). There is no avoidance of sensitive issues, no no-go areas. Jesus cuts to the quick. He is aware that the conversation is leading the woman to a place of vulnerability, but it is also a place of honesty and reality.

7 Jesus teaches her. He gives theological input over the issue of true worship (vv. 23, 24).

8 Jesus empowers her. While the conversation reveals the woman's weakness and need, it also equips her and gives her confidence to proclaim the saviour of the world. She is able to become a powerful witness to her community. As Kathleen Fischer puts it: 'Jesus calls her from the margin to the centre of life, from someone judged unworthy by the tradition, to a role as bearer of revelation to her community.'[8]

- How far do you identify with the eight approaches used by Jesus here?
- Put yourself in the woman's shoes. What transitions are taking place?

6 Climbing the mountain of encounter: Sherpa guide

The image of spiritual director suggested by the mountain is that of the Sherpa guides from Tibet and Nepal, famous for the remarkable assistance they give to mountaineering expeditions in the Himalayas, including the ascent of Mount Everest. These mountain guides are hardy, experienced and skilled. They know the joys and dangers of the ascent and descent. They have trod this way many times before and have come to an understanding of the terrain, its beauty and risks. They know where there are hazardous and slippery paths; they watch out for signs of altitude sickness in the climbers; they walk beside the explorer and help carry the load and share the burden. Sherpas are keenly aware that they tread on sacred ground – the mountain is a holy place to be approached with awe and respect, not to be 'conquered'. Theirs is a costly ministry, for they are not immune from the dangers of the mountain or from the risk of slipping.[9]

This vivid image of the spiritual director resonates with the spiritual journey as *ascesis* or training (compare Paul's picture of the spiritual athlete in 1 Cor. 9.24–27).

- In what way do you see the role of the spiritual director as a coach or mentor?
- Which spiritual disciplines have helped you most in the ascent?

7 Discovering the forgotten threshold: doorkeeper

The man born blind, eyes blinking in the sunlight as he emerges from the mighty Pool of Siloam, sees the inviting staircase that clings to the side of the Ophel ridge and begins his ascent to the Temple sanctuary from which he has been barred all his life. The steps lead to the Hulda Gate of the Temple and the first person he meets is the doorkeeper – a powerful image of the spiritual director who is ushering people across the threshold of prayer into a greater awareness of God's presence. Perhaps our rejected man-turned-pilgrim recalled Psalm 84:

How lovely is your dwelling place,
O Lord of hosts!
My soul longs, indeed it faints
for the courts of the Lord. (vv. 1–2)

The psalm goes on:

I would rather be a doorkeeper in the house of my God
than live in the tents of wickedness. (v. 10)

The New Jerusalem Bible translates verse 10 as 'Better . . . to stand on the threshold of God's house.' The image suggested to us is of one who lingers on the *limen* of the Temple sanctuary area, ready to welcome the pilgrim or searcher into the arena of the sacred, the domain of the holy. This is not an officious security officer – as might be found today on the Temple Mount – needing to control admittance into the Temple area. Rather it is a role whose origins can be traced back to the earliest days of the First Temple – doorkeepers were a sacred order mentioned in the books of Chronicles, Ezra and Nehemiah (a detailed description is given in 1 Chron. 9.17–32). The role is described as an 'office of trust'. A key function was to unlock and open up the gates each new day and welcome pilgrims into the holy area: 'they would spend the night near the house of God; for on them lay the duty of watching, and they had charge of opening it every morning' (1 Chron. 9.27). As our newly sighted pilgrim made his first-ever entry into the Temple area, the doorkeeper was perhaps taken aback to see him – where had he been all this time?

As a doorkeeper to the sacred, the spiritual director is not in the business of judging the status of others but of enabling and assisting their passage and approach to the holy. How many, like our pilgrim in the story of John 9, hang back out of a sense of unworthiness or self-denigration? This may come either from a false view of the self – as unclean and unfit to approach God; or from a false view of God – as one who principally judges or punishes. The role of the director as doorkeeper is to assure the pilgrim-seeker that the door to God's presence swings wide open for them. The Letter to the Hebrews urges us:

Therefore, my friends, since we have confidence to enter the sanctuary by the blood of Jesus, by the new and living way that he opened for us through the curtain (that is, through his flesh), and since we have a great high priest over the house of God, let us approach with a true heart in full assurance of faith, with our hearts sprinkled clean from an evil conscience and our bodies washed with pure water.

(Heb. 10.19–22)

This reminds us that the Pool of Siloam, through which the pilgrim waded, prefigures for us the waters of baptism, which declare to us that we are accepted, honoured and cherished by God as his beloved sons and daughters. It is the role of the spiritual director to provide a context and environment of patient listening to the directee that speaks of reassurance and confidence-building as we approach the Holy of Holies in prayer.

- In your experience, what holds people back from a closer encounter with God?
- How would you go about encouraging such people to cross the threshold to the holy?

8 Ascending towards the holy city: liberator

In the narrative of John 11 there seem to be at least two processes of liberation at work. The most obvious, of course, is the liberation of Lazarus from death and the tomb. Jesus seeks helpers: he commands those at hand: 'Unbind him, and let him go!' (v. 44). The helpers assist in the unbinding of Lazarus, taking off the strips of burial shroud that imprison him, releasing him from his captivity. But there is a second work of liberation going on, and it is taking place in the hearts of Martha and Mary. Martha in particular is being liberated, by stages, from constricting views of prayer. As we take another look at this, the role of the spiritual director emerges as liberator. Immediately, of course, we respond to this idea with the reaction that God is the only liberator. But there is a role for directors to help untie the bonds that constrain, to help unbind him – or her – and let them go. We need to be able to recognize what is tightening the spiritual life, what is becoming constrictive.

Martha is released, as we have seen, from her crippling but persistent views of prayer in relation to intercession, or bringing the needs of others to God. The problem is that all three views are respectable and traditional.

First, we noticed, she is learning that intercession is about surrender, not control. In the face of Lazarus' illness she sends out an urgent plea to Jesus. It is not spelt out but it carries the force: 'come and heal my brother, and do it quickly!' (cf. v. 3). This is ultimately a manipulative and prescriptive type of prayer that wishes not only to give advice to God but also tells God what to do. That this was her intent is revealed in her later comment, also repeated by Mary: 'if you had been here, my brother would not have died' (11.21, 32). This type of prayer springs from a heart that wants to regain control and mastery over a deteriorating situation. It seeks a favour to alleviate things. It is common today in many expressions of intercession, public and private, but it misses the heart of intercession, which is to let go of our control and heavy grip on a situation and move to a place of trust and submission where God can start to work on *us*. Martha's default type of intercession seeks to let us off the hook and avoid our responsibility as members of the body of Christ. The role of the director here may involve seeking to identify why a person needs to stay 'in control' at all times – what insecurities does this reveal? The role is to loosen the straps of this type of prayer and nudge the person towards seeing that intercession is really inseparable from self-offering and self-exposure to the possibilities of God's glory bubbling up wherever *God* chooses.

The second transition taking place in the sisters is related to this: it is from seeing Jesus in functionalist terms – here as a successful miracle worker – to seeing him in more mysterious terms that respect his sovereignty and awesomeness. Directors must remain alert to what image of God is in view in directees. Are they trying to tie God down into a manageable box or category? How far are they prepared for the risk of seeing God as inexplicable, inscrutable, indefinable and unpredictable? Martha's first prayer excluded the possibility that Jesus might weep alongside her. She wanted an efficient saviour who would come and do this expected business and more or less leave them alone after that. Such is the transformation in her sister Mary, at the sight of the tears of Jesus, that she is moved to an outrageous act of impetuous personal generosity, for soon she will pour ointment over his feet (John 12.1–8). She has been changed forever by the transition narrated in John 11. This is about opening up to a greater God and being released from the confines of narrow thinking about God.

A third transition, we noted, is a liberation from respectable but distancing dogma in order to embrace the surprises of God. Martha moves from an idea of a remote last day to the reality of resurrection breaking out now. It is easier, perhaps, to have a set of credal beliefs that don't impinge too much on us: they are less threatening than the idea that God might be on the doorstep or even within us by his Spirit. They keep God at arm's length. The liberating role of the spiritual director here is in exploring what most impacts on our spiritual experience; how far we are prepared for the vulnerability of encounter; what barriers or defence mechanisms are erected to keep God at bay. This is a truly liberating ministry: unbinding the tightened, defensive soul; loosening one from dogma, if this has become a way of keeping God at a safe distance.

- What is your experience of helping to liberate someone from constrictive views of God or prayer?
- What would you say to someone who has become entrapped or entangled in dogma?

9 Passing over: midwife

Jesus employs the image of a birth taking place in relation to the disciples participating in the paschal mystery. On the eve of his passion he says to them:

> you will have pain, but your pain will turn into joy. When a woman is in labour, she has pain, because her hour has come. But when her child is born, she no longer remembers the

anguish because of the joy of having brought a human being into the world. So you have pain now; but I will see you again, and your hearts will rejoice. (John 16.20–22)

Jesus refers to the tumultuous events to come as 'This is but the beginning of the birth pangs' (Mark 13.8). As we have seen, Paul says 'the whole creation has been groaning in labour pains until now' (Rom. 8.22). Paschal transitions resemble childbirth in several ways.[10] Fundamentally, there is the demanding experience of letting go and embracing new beginnings – the devastation of loss and the exhilaration of gain. This may be accompanied by struggle and resistance, by fear and helplessness, the lack of a sense of being 'in charge'. The role of the spiritual director as midwife is essentially that of encouragement, of being there, staying there, in the chaos or pain of the birthing process. The key role is to give reassurance, or rather to mediate God's reassurance: 'all will be well, and all manner of things will be well'. Indeed, this image can be enriched by reference to Jesus' motherhood, as Julian of Norwich develops it:

> Our true Mother Jesus . . . carries us within him in love and travail, until the full time when he wanted to suffer the sharpest thorns and cruel pains that ever were . . . in our spiritual bringing to birth he uses more tenderness, without any comparison, in protecting us.[11]

- Which spiritual birthing have you been present at?
- What forms of support were most effective?

10 Reaching beyond limits

Travelling through the marginalized region of Galilee, Jesus understood himself to be a prophet (Mark 6.4; Luke 4.16–30), and this suggests a challenging model of spiritual direction. The burden of the Old Testament prophets was not prediction of the future, rather speaking God's word into the present situation, naming the idols and illusions of contemporary society. For example, Amos was concerned to deliver his people from self-satisfying rituals and self-absorbing forms of prayer and alert them to the desperate needs of the society around them: 'I hate, I despise your festivals . . . But let justice roll down like waters, and righteousness like an ever-flowing stream' (Amos 5.21, 24). In similar vein Isaiah is uncompromising: 'Is this not the fast that I choose: to loosen the bonds of injustice, to undo the thongs of the yoke, to let the oppressed go free . . . Is it not to share your bread with the hungry . . . ?' (Isa. 58.6–7).

The task of the spiritual director is at times to point the person towards the forgotten ones of Galilee. Two images come to mind: hands uplifted in prayer must become hands outstretched in care; holy hands become dirty, bruised, wounded. And we have two ears: one to listen to God, one to listen to the cries of the poor, the screams of the exploited – which might turn out to be the cry of God himself.

The spiritual director must be prepared to ask searching questions of the person's prayer life and lifestyle. Are there danger signs that this person's spirituality is becoming narcissistic, self-centred, closed in on itself? Is this spirituality about self-fulfilment or about empowering sacrificial living? If the measure of spiritual maturity is increasing solidarity with the hurting, an enlarging capacity for compassion, what are the signs that this person is maturing? Is his or her heart getting bigger? Can this person allow the pain of the world to enter his or her prayer? Does this prayer have room for the oppressions and injustices of the world? What place is there in this person for costly intercession, open to the wider world? Indeed, what is this person's understanding of intercession? Is it, as we saw in Martha above, about advising God or rather, in Michael Ramsey's memorable phrase, 'coming before God with the people on your heart'? What place is there in this person's prayer for the cross – not only in terms of seeking personal forgiveness but in realizing that God suffers? What does Matthew 25 look like in this person's experience? What is the evidence? A 'time to keep silence, and a time to speak' (Eccles. 3.7): is this balance revealed in this person? How is this person living the challenge to be a contemplative in action? How is he or she finding God in *all* things?

In this prophetic role, the spiritual director needs to help the pray-er to stay in vital touch with God's longings for the wider world. Walter Brueggemann, in his classic work *The Prophetic Imagination*,[12] tells us that the role of the prophet is to open up for people a different vision of things: this is what Jesus does in his teaching about the kingdom of God, which questions the prevailing status quo represented by the kingdom of Rome. The role of the prophet is to suggest an alternative perspective that may be both subversive and compassionate, revealing itself in countercultural lifestyle and political choices.

'He is going ahead of you to Galilee; there you will see him.' The director must remind the person that the risen Christ he or she seeks is to be found in the margins.

- How would you go about broaching the subject of seeking Jesus in the despised?
- What is your own experience of finding God in the dust and dirt?

Notes

Introduction

1 See Mark 8.27; 9.33–34; 10.17, 32, 52; 11.8.
2 A. Van Gennep, *The Rites of Passage* (London: Routledge, 2010).
3 V. Turner, *The Ritual Process: Structure and Anti-structure* (New York: Aldine Transaction, 1995). He explores pilgrimage as a liminal experience in V. Turner and E. Turner, *Image and Pilgrimage in Christian Culture: Anthropological Perspectives* (New York: Columbia University Press, 1995).
4 S. Hauerwas and W. H. Willimon, *Resident Aliens* (Nashville, TN: Abingdon Press, 1989).
5 I am grateful to my colleague Sue Cash, fellow teacher on a training course for spiritual directors, for reading the manuscript and for her helpful suggestions.
6 In Year 3 of Lent the pattern is: 1 desert; 2 transfiguration; 3 Samaria; 4 Siloam; 5 Lazarus. Chapters 8–10 might form the basis of Holy Week homilies in any year.

1 Wading across the river

1 Luke tell us that Jesus attended the Temple at age 12, but he probably made regular visits, as in John's Gospel. The three annual festivals were Passover (Pesach), Pentecost (Shavout) and Tabernacles (Sukkoth).
2 C. A. Redmount, 'Bitter Lives: Israel in and out of Egypt', in M. D. Coogan (ed.), *The Oxford History of the Biblical World* (Oxford: Oxford University Press, 1999).
3 W. Bridges, *Transitions: Making Sense of Life's Changes* (Cambridge, MA: Da Capo Press, 2004), chapter 6 or pp. 133–55.
4 This resonates with the story in Genesis 32 of Jacob struggling with God in the waters of the Jabbok. See A. D. Mayes, *Spirituality of Struggle: Pathways to Growth* (London: SPCK, 2002). For further exploration of the transitions into ministry, see A. D. Mayes, *Spirituality in Ministerial Formation: The Dynamic of Prayer in Learning* (Cardiff: University of Wales Press, 2009), to which this paragraph is indebted.

5 See I. Matthew, *The Impact of God: Soundings from St John of the Cross* (London: Hodder & Stoughton, 1995), p. 72.

6 K. Kavanaugh and O. Rodriguez (trs), *The Collected Works of St John of the Cross* (Washington, DC: ICS, 1991), p. 177.

7 Stages of development in Christian spirituality are represented in the pioneering work of the psychologists Erik Erikson and James W. Fowler. See E. H. Erikson, *Childhood and Society* (Harmondsworth: Pelican, 1969) and *Identity and the Life Cycle* (New York and London: Norton, 1994); and J. W. Fowler, *Stages of Faith: The Psychology of Human Development and the Quest for Meaning* (San Francisco: Harper, rev. edn, 1995). For a recent reworking of the Triple Way in the psychology of spirituality, see B. J. Groeschel, *Spiritual Passages: The Psychology of Spiritual Development* (New York: Crossroad, 1995). See also E. Liebert, *Changing Life Patterns: Adult Development in Spiritual Direction* (St Louis, MO: Chalice Press, 2000).

8 R. Williams, *Teresa of Avila* (London: Continuum, 1991), pp. 113, 114.

9 A. Peers (tr.), *St Teresa of Avila: Interior Castle* (London: Sheed & Ward, 1974), pp. 6, 8. See a recent translation in K. Kavanaugh and O. Rodriguez (trs), *Teresa of Avila: The Interior Castle* (New York: Paulist Press, 1979).

10 C. Humphreys, *From Ash to Fire: A Contemporary Journey through the Interior Castle of Teresa of Avila* (New York: New City Press, 1992), p. 80.

11 Peers, *St Teresa of Avila: Interior Castle*, p. 33.

12 Peers, *St Teresa of Avila: Interior Castle*, p. 55.

13 T. Bielecki, *Teresa of Avila: An Introduction to her Life and Writings* (Tunbridge Wells: Burns & Oates, 1994), p. 115.

14 Peers, *St Teresa of Avila: Interior Castle*, p. 148.

15 Kavanaugh and Rodriguez, *Teresa of Avila: The Interior Castle*, p. 42.

16 Kavanaugh and Rodriguez, *Teresa of Avila: The Interior Castle*, p. 36.

17 The Archbishops' Council, *Common Worship: Christian Initiation* (London: Church House Publishing, 2006).

18 From 'Parochial and Plain Sermons', viii, in E. Przywara (ed.), *The Heart of Newman* (Wheathampstead: Anthony Clarke, 1963).

2 Advancing through desert margins

1 G. A. Maloney (tr.), *Intoxicated with God: The Fifty Spiritual Homilies of Macarius* (Denville, NJ: Dimension Books, 1978).

2 B. Ward (tr.), *The Sayings of the Desert Fathers: The Alphabetical Collection* (Kalamazoo, MI: Cistercian, 1975), p. 87.

3 Ward, *Sayings of the Desert Fathers*, p. 3.

4 Ward, *Sayings of the Desert Fathers*, p. 86.

5 Ward, *Sayings of the Desert Fathers*, p. 30.

6 Ward, *Sayings of the Desert Fathers*, p. 139.

7 See S. Rubenson, *The Letters of St Anthony: Monasticism and the Making of a Saint* (Minneapolis, MN: Fortress Press, 1995), p. 59.

8 'Letter 3', in Rubenson, *Letters of St Anthony*, p. 206.

9 T. Merton, *The Wisdom of the Desert* (Boston and London: Shambhala, 1960), pp. 4, 7.

10 H. Nouwen, *The Way of the Heart* (London: Darton, Longman & Todd, 1987), pp. 27, 32.

11 Ward, *Sayings of the Desert Fathers*, p. 230.

12 Ward, *Sayings of the Desert Fathers*, p. 234.

13 Ward, *Sayings of the Desert Fathers*, p. 95.

14 Ward, *Sayings of the Desert Fathers*, p. 103.

15 Ward, *Sayings of the Desert Fathers*, p. 104.

16 Ward, *Sayings of the Desert Fathers*, p. 97.

17 R. Rohr, *Everything Belongs: The Gift of Contemplative Prayer* (New York: Crossroad, 2003), p. 97.

3 Venturing to the coastlands

1 We must also remember how the telling of this story has been shaped by the context and needs of its first readership: Matthew was writing for Jewish Christians, Mark was addressing attitudes among his Gentile community.

2 See R. Rohr, *The Naked Now: Learning to See as the Mystics See* (New York: Crossroad, 2009) and C. Bourgeault, *The Wisdom Jesus: Transforming Heart and Mind – A New Perspective on Christ and his Message* (Boston: Shambhala, 2008).

3 R. Horsley, *Jesus and Empire: The Kingdom of God and the New World Disorder* (Minneapolis, MN: Fortress Press, 2002).

4 E. H. Cousins, *Bonaventure and the Coincidence of Opposites* (Chicago: Franciscan Herald Press, 1978).

5 Rohr, *Naked Now*, p. 77.

6 Luke 5.8, *Holy Bible: God's Word Translation* (Iowa Falls, IA: World Publishing, 1995).

7 From 'Hymn on Faith, 10', in S. P. Brock, *The Luminous Eye: The Spiritual World Vision of St Ephrem the Syrian* (Kalamazoo, MI: Cistercian, 1992), pp. 40, 108. The three extracts from St Ephrem are Copyright

1992 by Cistercian Publications and published by Liturgical Press, Collegeville, MN. Reprinted with permission. See also S. P. Brock, *Spirituality in the Syriac Tradition* (Kottayam, India: SEERI, 2005).

8 'Hymn on Faith, 3', in Brock, *Luminous Eye*, p. 73.

9 'Hymn on the Church, 29', in Brock, *Luminous Eye*, p. 75.

10 T. J. Samuelian (tr.), *St Grigor Narekatsi: Speaking with God from the Depths of the Heart* (Yerevan, Armenia: Vem Press, 2002); M. Kudian (tr.), *Nerses Shnorhali: Jesus the Son* (London: Mashtots Press, 1986).

11 Matthew the Poor, *Orthodox Prayer Life: The Interior Way* (New York: St Vladimir's Seminary Press, 2003).

12 G. E. H. Palmer, P. Sherrard and K. Ware (trs), *The Philokalia* (London: Faber & Faber, vol. 1: 1979, vol. 2: 1981).

13 Sayings from I. Gorainov, *The Message of Saint Seraphim* (Oxford: Fairacres Publications, 2007). See also S. Bolshakoff, *Russian Mystics* (Kalamazoo, MI: Cistercian, 1976).

14 See Simeon New Theologian, *On the Mystical Life: The Ethical Discourses* (New York: St Vladimir's Seminary Press, 1996).

15 J. S. Pobee, 'African Spirituality', in G. S. Wakefield (ed.), *The SCM Dictionary of Christian Spirituality* (London: SCM Press, 1983), p. 8.

16 From A. Shorter, *African Christian Spirituality* (Maryknoll, NY: Orbis, 1980), p. 107; quoted with permission.

17 P. Casaldaliga and J. M. Vigil, *The Spirituality of Liberation* (Tunbridge Wells: Burns & Oates, 1994), p. xxvii. See also G. Gutiérrez, *We Drink from Our Own Wells* (London: SCM Press, 1984).

18 Peter Dronke, quoted in F. Bowie and O. Davies (eds), *Hildegard of Bingen: An Anthology* (London: SPCK, 1990), p. 3.

19 Bowie and Davies, *Hildegard of Bingen*, p. 32.

20 M. Buber, *I and Thou* (London: Continuum, 2004).

21 See, for example, J. M. Stoutzenberger and J. D. Bohrer, *Praying with Francis of Assisi* (Winona, MA: Saint Mary's Press, 1989).

22 Popularized by Basil Pennington and Thomas Keating and promoted by Contemplative Outreach. See M. B. Pennington, *Centering Prayer: Renewing an Ancient Christian Prayer Form* (Garden City, NY: Doubleday, 1980); T. Keating, *Intimacy with God: An Introduction to Centering Prayer* (New York: Crossroad, 2009).

23 *The Call of the Minaret* (Oxford: Oxford University Press, 1956); *Muhammad and the Christian* (London: Darton, Longman & Todd, 1984); *Muhammad in the Qur'an: The Task and the Text* (London: Melisende, 2001).

24 Abhishiktananda, *Hindu-Christian Meeting Point: Within the Cave of the Heart* (Delhi: ISPCK, 1983). See also D. Forster, *An Uncommon Spiritual Path: The Quest to find Jesus Beyond Conventional Christianity* (Kempton Park, South Africa: AcadSA Publishers, 2008).

25 Back cover, Abhishiktananda, *Saccidananda: A Christian Approach to Advaitic Experience* (Delhi: ISPCK, 2007).

26 B. Griffiths, *The Marriage of East and West* (Tucson, AZ: Medio Media, 2003).

27 As explored with Zen Master Suzuki in *Zen and the Birds of Appetite* (New York: New Directions, 1968).

28 Quoted in W. H. Shannon, *Something of a Rebel: Thomas Merton, his Life and Works* (Cincinnati, OH: St Anthony Messenger Press, 1997), p. 167. See T. Merton, *Asian Journey* (New York: New Directions, 1973).

29 T. Merton, *The Monastic Journey* (London: Sheldon Press, 1977), p. 3.

4 Traversing the risky lake

1 See, for example, J. Monbourquette, *How to Befriend Your Shadow: Welcoming your Unloved Side* (London: Darton, Longman & Todd, 2001).

2 The title of John V. Taylor's classic work on the Holy Spirit (London: SCM Press, 1972).

3 'The Great God of Heaven', hymn by H. R. Bramley (1833–1917). See also the Nativity hymns of the Orthodox Church in Mother Mary and Kallistos Ware (trs), *The Festal Menaion* (London: Faber & Faber, 1977), and for a modern example, Graham Kendrick's hymn 'Meekness and Majesty'.

4 Fifteenth Antiphon of Good Friday Matins, in Mother Mary and Kallistos Ware (trs), *The Lenten Triodion* (South Canaan, PA: St. Tikhon's Seminary Press, 1994), pp. 565ff.; quoted with permission.

5 C. Smith, *The Way of Paradox* (London: Collins, 1987), p. 27.

6 Smith, *Way of Paradox*, p. 26.

7 M. Fox (tr.), *Meditations with Meister Eckhart* (Rochester, VT: Bear & Company, 1983), p. 49. <www.InnerTraditions.com>. Reprinted with permission. For a useful anthology, see U. Fleming (ed.), *Meister Eckhart: The Man from whom God hid Nothing* (London: Collins/Fount, 1988).

8 Fox, *Meditations with Meister Eckhart*, p. 110.

9 According to the biography by Izaak Walton, *The Lives of John Donne, Sir Henry Wotton, Richard Hooker, George Herbert, and Robert Sanderson* (London: Oxford University Press, 1927).

10 See, for example, Psalms 22, 42.

11 From the 'The Cross', in F. E. Hutchinson (ed.), *The Works of George Herbert* (Oxford: Clarendon Press, 1970). See also A. D. Mayes, *Spirituality of Struggle: Pathways to Growth* (London: SPCK, 2002) and P. Sheldrake, *Love Took My Hand: The Spirituality of George Herbert* (London: Darton, Longman & Todd, 2000).

12 Poems available on <www.ccel.org>.

5 Penetrating Samaria's border

1 It is not always possible to know whether these derive from Jesus himself or reflect the situation faced by the Christian communities for whom the Gospels were first written.

2 Though the reference to the Spirit is not explicit here, the imagery of water and Spirit is a key theme in John's Gospel (John 3, 7).

3 See, for example, N. T. Wright, *Jesus and the Victory of God* (London: SPCK, 1996). Also M. Coloe, *God Dwells with Us: Temple Symbolism in the Fourth Gospel* (Collegeville, MN: Liturgical Press, 2001). But as we shall see in Chapter 7, Jesus still allows a role for the Temple.

4 This raises an interesting debate in relation to Christians and holy places: should we continue to seek God in holy places? See A. D. Mayes, *Holy Land? Challenging Questions from the Biblical Landscape* (London: SPCK, 2011), ch. 1. See also P. Walker, *Holy City, Holy Places? Christian Attitudes to Jerusalem and the Holy Land in the Fourth Century* (Oxford: Clarendon Press, 1990).

5 See the research reported in S. Croft et al., *Evangelism in a Spiritual Age* (London: Church House Publishing, 2005).

6 J. Moltmann, *The Spirit of Life: A Universal Affirmation* (London: SCM Press, 1992), p. 200.

7 J. Macquarrie, *Paths in Spirituality* (London: SCM Press, 1972), p. 34.

8 R. Williams, *Teresa of Avila* (London: Continuum, 1991), p. 156.

9 F. Watts and M. Williams, *The Psychology of Religious Knowing* (London: Chapman, 1988), p. 115.

10 Watts and Williams, *Psychology of Religious Knowing*, p. 113.

11 A. Ulanov and B. Ulanov, *Primary Speech: A Psychology of Prayer* (Atlanta: John Knox, 1982), p. 122. See also experiences of God

as understood as perception in W. P. Alson, *Perceiving God: The Epistemology of Religious Experience* (Ithaca, NY and London: Cornell University Press, 1991).

12 There is an Israeli population in these hills – the settlements – with an alternative network of brand-new roads that only Israeli settlers can use; Palestinian locals are barred from them.

6 Climbing the mountain of encounter

1 Mount Tabor (1,800 feet) became established as the place visited by pilgrims since the fourth century, because of its handy proximity to Nazareth.

2 J. D. G. Dunn, *Jesus Remembered* (Grand Rapids, MI/Cambridge: Eerdmans, 2003), p. 56.

3 J. Borysenko, in her *A Woman's Journey to God* (New York: Riverhead/ Penguin, 2001), contrasts male spirituality represented in the ascent model of Jacob's ladder, with its successive linear stages, with female spirituality symbolized in Sarah's circle, a more relational, immanent model: less climbing, more nurturing!

4 For a critique of the ascent model, see M. Miles, *The Image and Practice of Holiness* (London: SCM Press, 1989).

5 'Letter 2', in G. Barrois (tr.), *The Fathers Speak* (New York: St Vladimir's Seminary Press, 1986).

6 V. Lossky, *The Mystical Theology of the Eastern Church* (London: James Clarke, 1957), p. 223.

7 E. Cousins (tr.), *Bonaventure: The Soul's Journey into God* (New York: Paulist Press, 1978), p. 89.

8 Ignatius of Loyola invites us to use our five senses to trigger our imaginations as we engage with the text – A. Mottola (tr.), *The Spiritual Exercises of St Ignatius* (New York: Image/Doubleday, 1964).

9 It begins with baptism, prefigured in the crossing of the Red Sea, liberating a person from the captivity not of Pharaoh but of sin. The Christian pilgrim's journey, like the trek through the wilderness, will be marked by God's provision (as in manna, water from the rock), God's guidance (the pillar of cloud), human failure and spiritual battles (as represented in the conflict with Amalekites). See A. J. Malherbe and E. Ferguson (trs), *Gregory of Nyssa: The Life of Moses* (New York: Paulist Press, 1978), II:226.227, p. 113.

10 See 'On Perfection', in H. Musurillo (tr.), *From Glory to Glory* (New York: St Vladimir's Seminary Press, 2001), pp. 51–52. See also A. Louth,

The Origins of the Christian Mystical Tradition (Oxford: Oxford University Press, 2007).

11 P. Chandler (ed.), *A Journey with Elijah* (Rome: Carmelite Institute, 1991), p. 112.

12 Malherbe and Ferguson, *Gregory of Nyssa: The Life of Moses*, p. 92.

13 Malherbe and Ferguson, *Gregory of Nyssa: The Life of Moses*, p. 95.

14 All quotations are from C. Wolters (tr.), *The Cloud of Unknowing* (London: Penguin, 1976), here pp. 53, 54. For a more recent translation, see J. Walsh (tr.), *The Cloud of Unknowing* (New York: Paulist Press, 1981). See also D. Lonsdale, 'The Cloud of Unknowing', in L. Byrne (ed.), *Traditions of Spiritual Guidance* (Collegeville, MN: Liturgical Press, 1990).

15 Wolters, *Cloud of Unknowing*, p. 60.

16 Wolters, *Cloud of Unknowing*, p. 51. For a consideration of the role of desire in spirituality, see P. Sheldrake, *Befriending Our Desires* (London: Darton, Longman & Todd, 1994).

17 Wolters, *Cloud of Unknowing*, p. 110.

18 Wolters, *Cloud of Unknowing*, p. 61.

19 See note 3 above.

7 Discovering the forgotten threshold

1 J. Murphy-O'Connor, *The Holy Land: The Indispensable Archaeological Guide for Travellers* (Oxford: Oxford University Press, 1992), p. 121.

2 For scholarly articles, see R. Reich, E. Shukron and O. Lernau, 'Recent Discoveries in the City of David, Jerusalem', *Israel Exploration Journal*, vol. 57 no. 2 (2007), pp. 153–168; Doron Ben-Ami and Yana Tchekhanovets, 'The Lower City of Jerusalem on the Eve of its Destruction, 70 C.E.: A View from Hanyon Givati', *Bulletin of the American Schools of Oriental Research*, no. 364 (Nov. 2011), pp. 61–85.

3 The other half lies under an orchard in Greek Orthodox property. This is a controversial dig because it is in occupied East Jerusalem and associated with the City of David Archaeological Park, which has displaced several Palestinian families from their homes in the Arab village of Silwan (its name is derived from Siloam). With the proposed creation of the 'King's Garden' here, further homes are to be requisitioned and demolished.

4 The Archbishops' Council, *Common Worship: Christian Initiation* (London: Church House Publishing, 2006).

5 *Common Worship: Christian Initiation.*
6 *Common Worship: Christian Initiation.*
7 John links the gift of the Spirit to the paschal mystery. At the crucifixion, a fountain of eternal life is opened for humanity: as his side is pierced, blood and water stream out (John 19.34; cf. 1 John 5.6–8). After Jesus is glorified on the cross, the Spirit can gush.
8 'The Water Drawing Ceremony' from <www.lchaimweekly.org>.
9 *Common Worship: Christian Initiation.*

8 Ascending towards the holy city

1 In his exploration of the mountains in Matthew's Gospel, Terence Donaldson notes a link between the Mount of Olives and the mount of commissioning in Galilee, with the recurring phrase 'the end of the age' (cf. 24.3 and 28.20) – T. L. Donaldson, *Jesus on the Mountain: A Study in Matthean Theology* (Sheffield: JSOT Press, 1985).
2 For an archaeological perspective on the story, see S. Gibson, *The Final Days of Jesus: The Archaeological Evidence* (New York: HarperOne, 2009). For a dramatic re-imagining, see R. Beard, *Lazarus is Dead* (London: Vintage, 2012).
3 For an overview of scholarship on John's Gospel, see G. S. Sloyan, *What Are They Saying About John?* (New York: Paulist Press, 2006).
4 For an excellent reflection on intercession, see J. N. Ward, *The Use of Praying* (London: Epworth Press, 1967).
5 See S. M. Schneiders, 'The Resurrection (of the Body) in the Fourth Gospel', in J. R. Donahue (ed.), *Life in Abundance: Studies of John's Gospel in Tribute to Raymond E. Brown* (Collegeville, MN: Liturgical Press, 2005).

9 Passing over

1 From the Holy Week hymn 'Pascha Nostrum' (cf. 1 Cor. 5.7–8) – *Book of Common Prayer of the Episcopal Church*, 1979.
2 R. Rolheiser, *Seeking Spirituality: Guidelines for a Christian Spirituality for the Twenty-First Century* (London: Hodder & Stoughton, 1998), p. 137.
3 The Synoptic Gospels give clues that the Last Supper is a Passover celebration.
4 J. Jeremias, *The Eucharistic Words of Jesus* (London: SCM Press, 1966), p. 223; emphasis in original.

5 R. Foster, *Prayer: Finding the Heart's True Home* (London: Hodder & Stoughton, 1992).

6 K. Muggeridge (tr.), *The Sacrament of the Present Moment: Jean-Pierre de Caussade* (London: Fount, 1996). He sought to counter the heresy of Quietism, which taught that the surest way to union with God was to foster a state of utter passivity before God, necessitating a complete withdrawal from the world, the annihilation of the human will and a cessation of all human effort, in the search to become totally available to God.

7 Rom. 8.28, NRSV textual variant.

8 Muggeridge, *Sacrament of the Present Moment*, p. 46.

9 Muggeridge, *Sacrament of the Present Moment*, p. 75.

10 Muggeridge, *Sacrament of the Present Moment*, p. 40.

11 Muggeridge, *Sacrament of the Present Moment*, p. 54.

12 Muggeridge, *Sacrament of the Present Moment*, p. 109.

13 See John 18.4ff.

14 I am indebted for this insight to S. H. Lee, *From a Liminal Place: An Asian American Theology* (Minneapolis, MN: Fortress Press, 2010).

15 J. Follent, 'Negative Experience and Christian Growth', in P. Slattery (ed.), *St John of the Cross* (New York: Alba House, 1994), p. 97.

16 Ronald Knox's translation of Galatians 2.20.

17 Romans 6.4, *Holy Bible: God's Word Translation* (Iowa Falls, IA: World Publishing, 1995).

10 Reaching beyond limits

1 S. Freyne, *Jesus, a Jewish Galilean: A New Reading of the Jesus Story* (London: T. & T. Clark, 2004); R. A. Horsley, *Archaeology, History and Society in Galilee: The Social Context of Jesus and the Rabbis* (Valley Forge, PA: Trinity Press International, 1995). See also J. Meier, *A Marginal Jew: Rethinking the Historical Jesus*, 3 vols (New York: Doubleday, 1991–2001).

2 S. Freyne, *Galilee, Jesus and the Gospels: Literary Approaches and Historical Investigations* (Philadelphia, PA: Fortress Press, 1988), p. 54.

3 S. H. Lee, *From a Liminal Place: An Asian American Theology* (Minneapolis, MN: Fortress Press, 2010), p. 47.

4 P. Casaldáliga and J. M. Vigil, *The Spirituality of Liberation* (Tunbridge Wells: Burns & Oates, 1994), p. 140.

5 G. Gutiérrez, *A Theology of Liberation* (London: SCM Press, 1973), p. 118.

6 R. J. Armstrong, J. A. W. Hellmann and W. J. Short (eds), *Francis of Assisi: Early Documents*, vol. 1 (New York: New City Press, 1999), p. 124.

7 Address of Bishop Francis Weston to the Anglo-Catholic Congress 1923, from <anglicanhistory.org>.

8 L. Boff, *Way of the Cross – Way of Justice* (New York: Orbis, 1980).

Appendix

1 See L. W. Countryman, *Living on the Border of the Holy: Renewing the Priesthood of All* (Harrisburg, PA: Morehouse, 1999).

2 Recently, attention has been directed to the Desert Mothers as an area of current research. See, for example, L. Swan, *The Forgotten Desert Mothers: Sayings, Lives, and Stories of Early Christian Women* (New York: Paulist Press, 2001). Cf. P. Brown, 'The Rise and Function of the Holy Man in Late Antiquity', *Journal of Roman Studies* (vol. 61, Nov. 1971), pp. 80–101.

3 K. Leech, *Soul Friend* (London: Sheldon Press, 1977), p. 43.

4 C. Luibheid (tr.), *John Cassian: Conferences* (New York: Paulist Press, 1985), p. 67.

5 Luibheid, *John Cassian: Conferences*, p. 62. See also J. Bertram (tr.), *Cassian: The Monastic Institutes* (London: Saint Austin Press, 1999).

6 Luibheid, *John Cassian: Conferences*, pp. 39, 41, 42.

7 C. Luibheid and N. Russell (trs), *John Climacus: The Ladder of Divine Ascent* (New York: Paulist Press, 1982), p. 259.

8 K. Fischer, *Women at the Well: Feminist Perspectives on Spiritual Direction* (London: SPCK, 1989), p. 47.

9 See Br Ramon ssf, *The Prayer Mountain: Exploring the High Places of Prayer* (Norwich: Canterbury Press, 1998).

10 This has been explored in M. Guenther, *Holy Listening: The Art of Spiritual Direction* (Cambridge, MA: Cowley Publications, 1992).

11 E. Colledge and J. Walsh (trs), *Julian of Norwich: Showings* (New York: Paulist Press, 1978), pp. 298, 299.

12 W. Brueggemann, *The Prophetic Imagination* (Minneapolis, MN: Fortress Press, rev. edn, 2001), chapter 2.